1978 SUPPLEMENT

to

PATENT LAW
FUNDAMENTALS

by

Peter D. Rosenberg

B.A., B.Ch.E., J.D., LL.M. (Patent & Trade Reg. Law)

Member, New York Bar
Examiner, U.S. Patent Office

Clark Boardman Company, Ltd.
New York, New York

Any opinions expressed in this work are those of the author and do not necessarily represent those of the U.S. Patent Office.

Library of Congress Catalog No. 74-15799

ISBN 0-87632-098-1

This is the first supplement to PATENT LAW FUNDAMEN-
TALS. To be used in conjunction with the main volume, this supplement updates the information contained there.

HOW TO USE THIS SUPPLEMENT

Most portions of the supplement are instructing you to add new
text (and accompanying footnotes) to existing text in the main
volume.

Example:

§ 1. Determination of Priority

§ 1[1]. Conception

PAGE 136

[*Add to text at end of section:*]

Conception involves not merely the perception or realization of
the desirability of producing a certain result. Rather, it involves the
perception or realization of means by which the result can be produced.[1.1]

[1.1] Bell Telephone Laboratories, Inc. v. Hughes Aircraft Co., 191 U.S.P.Q. 23, 29 (D.Del.
1976).

At other times, you are instructed to insert a footnote number into
the text where none now exists. You are then given the actual
footnote.

Example:

§ 4. Antitrust Analysis and Critique

PAGE 276

[*In fifth text line of first paragraph of the section, add footnote*
45.1 *after* "relation.":]

[45.1] Moraine Products v. ICI America, Inc., 538 F.2d 134, 146, 191 U.S.P.Q. 65, 75 (7th
Cir. 1976).

Finally, at the end of each chapter of the supplement, you will find a list of cases. These citations are simply to be added to footnotes which already exist; usually, these cases have been decided since publication of the main volume.

Example:

Notes

PAGE 282

[*Add to footnote* 1:]

Western Electric Co. v. Milgo Electronic Corp., 190 U.S.P.Q. 546 (S.D.Fla. 1976).

PAGE 283

[*Add to footnote* **54**:]

Zenith Laboratories, Inc. v. Carter-Wallace, Inc., 530 F.2d 508, 514, 189 U.S.P.Q. 387, 392 (3d Cir. 1976).

Note: In this supplement, the words "full paragraph," as distinguished from simply "paragraph," refer to a text paragraph which begins and ends on the same page.

Chapter 1

WHAT A PATENT IS

§ 2. A Patent as a Grant; As a Contract

PAGE 7

[*In 19th text line, delete all text after* "to the public.["] *and substitute:*]

The policy of the United States patent laws is that one who has invested time and labor in developing a new product shall have the benefit of his invention, by being given the right to exclude others completely from the enjoyment of his invention.[7.1] The consideration of quid pro quo[8] which is given the public is the prompt disclosure of a heretofore unknown inventon. The purpose of disclosure to the public is to catalyze other inventors into activity and make possible additional advances in the art.[8.1] The inventor makes a truly Faustian bargain with the sovereign, exchanging secrecy, of indefinite and of possibly perpetual duration, for ephemeral patent rights.

[7.1] Western Electric Co. v. Milgo Electronic Corp., 190 U.S.P.Q. 546, 549 (S.D. Fla. 1976).
[8] See, for example, Flick-Reedy Corp. v. Hydro-Line Mfg. Co., 351 F.2d 546, 551, 146 U.S.P.Q. 694, 697 (7th Cir. 1965).
[8.1] Ex parte Hall, 191 U.S.P.Q. 157, 159 (P.O.Bd.App. 1975).

§ 3. Patents as Monopolies and as (Intellectual) Property

PAGE 11

[*Add immediately preceding first full text paragraph on the page:*]

The holder of an improvement patent acquires no rights in the basic patent.[28.1]

[28.1] St. Regis Paper Co. v. Winchester Carton Corp., 410 F. Supp. 1304, 1308, 189 U.S.P.Q. 514, 517 (D. Mass. 1976).

PAGE 12

[*Add immediately preceding first full text paragraph on the page:*]

Paper patents must be strictly construed both as to validity and

1

infringement.[32.1] A paper patent may not be employed to establish the defense of "anticipation."[32.2]

[32.1] 189 U.S.P.Q. 649 (E.D. Mich. 1975).
[32.2] PPG Industries, Inc. v. Guardian Industries Corp., 191 U.S.P.Q. 719, 720 (N.D. Ohio 1976).

§ 5. Patents Are to Trade Secrets as a Right in Rem Is to a Right in Personam

PAGE 15

[*In fourth line of third text paragraph, add after* "as Coca Cola.":]

Moreover, prior art is a much less effective defense in a trade secret case than in a patent infringement case; novelty and invention are not essential for trade secret, as they are for patentability. That the general principle of the trade secret was known for many years is no defense to a claim of misappropriation of trade secret, where the subject of the trade was use and value of principle in a manner not before known.[50.1]

[50.1] Prince Mfg., Inc. v. Automatic Partner, Inc., 191 U.S.P.Q. 450, 459 (N.J.Sup.Ct. Chan. Div. Mercer City 1976).

PAGE 17

[*In tenth line of second complete text paragraph, add after* "issued.":]

While a prior ruling of patent validity does not create an estoppel of issues of fact against a person not before the court in the earlier case, it does substantially strengthen the statutory presumption of validity.[57.1]

[57.1] Illinois Tool Works, Inc. v. Foster Grant Co., 547 F.2d 1300, 1303, 192 U.S.P.Q. 365, 367 (7th Cir. 1976).

Notes

PAGE 20

Erratum: The correct citation for footnote **54** is:

[54] Metallizing Engineering Co. v. Kenyon Bearing & Auto Parts Co., 153 F.2d 516, 68 U.S.P.Q. 54 (2d Cir. 1946), *cert. denied* 328 U.S. 840, *rehearing denied* 328 U.S. 881 (1946).

Chapter 2

PATENTS, COPYRIGHTS, AND TRADEMARKS: SIGNIFICANT POINTS OF COMPARISON AND CONTRAST

PAGE 23

[*Following quoted matter at top of page, add to fourth line of text, after* "the other two.":]

Patent law does not ordinarily control copyright cases.[a1]

[a1] Granite Music Corp. v. United Artists Corp., 532 F.2d 718, 723, 189 U.S.P.Q. 406, 411 (9th Cir. 1976).

[*In 13th text line, add after* "certain formal requirements.":]

A patent may be infringed by innocent and independent reproduction, but independent creation of a copyrighted work does not constitute copyright infringement; nothing short of copying or plagiarism can infringe a copyright.[a2]

[a2] Granite Music Corp. v. United Artists Corp., 532 F.2d 718, 720, 189 U.S.P.Q. 406, 408 (9th Cir. 1976).

PAGE 24

[*After third text line in first full paragraph on the page, sentence now reads:*]

Similarly, under the Copyright Act of 1909 as amended, and prior federal copyright legislation, unless it has been registered with the Copyright Office,[5] state law controls the wrongful appropriation of an unpublished work, and an author's rights in such unpublished work are sometimes referred to as his common-law copyright.

[*In 21st text line of first full paragraph, insert after* "sanctioned":]

, in the absence of preemptive federal legislation,

PAGE 25

[*Add immediately preceding first full text paragraph on the page:*]

A new comprehensive Copyright Act, Public Law 94-553, was enacted on October 19, 1976. Most of its provisions will enter into force on January 1, 1978. The new law will supersede the Copyright Act of 1909, as amended. Instead of the present dual system of protecting works under state common law before they are published and under federal statute after publication, the new law will establish a single system of federal statutory protection for all copyrightable works, whether published or unpublished. For all works created after January 1, 1978 the new law's federal copyright protection will exist from the moment the work is created and will last for the author's life, plus an additional 50 years after the author's death. For works made for hire, and for anonymous and pseudonymous works, the new term will be 75 years from publication or 100 years from creation, whichever is shorter. For works already under statutory protection, the new law retains the present term of 28 years from first publication (or from registration for those unpublished works that were registrable and were registered under the Copyright Act of 1909), renewable by certain persons for a second period of protection, but it increases the length of the second period to 47 years. Copyrights in their first term must still be renewed to receive the full new maximum term of 75 years, but copyrights in their second term between December 31, 1976 and December 31, 1977, are automatically extended up to the maximum of 75 years without the need for further renewal. For unpublished works that are already in existence on January 1, 1978, but that are not protected by statutory copyright and have not yet gone into the public domain, the new Act will generally provide automatic federal copyright protection for the same life-plus-50 or 75/100-year terms prescribed for new works.

PAGE 29

[*In penultimate line of second full text paragraph, add before* "Trademark infringement":]

Moreover, because independent creation does not constitute copyright infringement, the copyright monopoly has been said to apply only to the reproduction of a work and not to its contents.[33.1]

[33.1] Granite Music Corp. v. United Artists Corp., 532 F.2d 718, 720, 189 U.S.P.Q. 406, 408 (9th Cir. 1976).

Chapter 3

PATENT CLAIMS

§ 2. Structural and Functional Language

PAGE 41

[*In third text line, add after* "need not describe it.[8]":]

The Court of Customs and Patent Appeals has stated that Section 112, second paragraph, is satisfied where the claims merely set out and circumscribe a particular area with a reasonable degree of precision and particularity.[8.1]

[8.1] *In re* Mercier, 515 F.2d 1161, 1168, 185 U.S.P.Q. 774, 780 (C.C.P.A. 1975).

[*Insert between first and second text paragraphs:*]

However, a claim reciting all the essential parts of a "kit" of parts, but not reciting the completed assembly, was held to be in compliance with the requirements of 35 U.S.C. 112, second paragraph.[10.1]

[10.1] *In re* Venezia, 530 F.2d 956, 189 U.S.P.Q. 149 (C.C.P.A. 1976).

§ 3. Phraseology of Claim

§ 3[1]. The Preamble or Introductory Phrase

PAGE 45

[*In last text line on the page, add after footnote* 22:]

Claimed structure that follows the preamble and is a self-contained description which does not depend for completeness on the introductory clause does not make the preamble limiting.[22.1] The significance accorded a preamble, however, is to be determined on the facts in each case. The preamble is to be considered when it gives life and meaning to recitations in the claims.[22.2] Thus, a U.S. district court construed a claim preamble as a limitation to the claim where it appeared that the preamble had been relied upon in the Patent Office to distinguish it over the prior art.[22.3]

[22.1] Ex parte Mott, 190 U.S.P.Q. 311 (P.O.Bd.App. 1975).

5

22.2 Ex parte Varga, 189 U.S.P.Q. 204 (P.O.Bd.App. 1973).

22.3 Jack Winter, Inc. v. Koratron Co., 375 F. Supp. 1, 20, 181 U.S.P.Q. 353, 361 (N.D. Cal. 1974).

§ 3[2]. Transitional Phrase

PAGE 46

[*Add footnote* **24.1** *at end of first paragraph in this section:*]

24.1 Lockheed Aircraft Corp. v. United States, 190 U.S.P.Q. 134, 144 (Ct.Cl. 1976).

[*Insert between third and fourth text paragraphs in this section:*]

The language "essentially consisting of" has been construed as being synonymous with "consisting essentially of."[26.1] A process or method "consisting essentially of" certain enumerated steps is to be construed in a manner analogous to a composition-of-matter claim "consisting essentially of" the ingredients enumerated.[26.2]

26.1 Ziegler v. Phillips, 483 F.2d 858, 177 U.S.P.Q. 481 (5th Cir. 1973).

26.2 Ex parte Volheim, 191 U.S.P.Q. 407 (P.O.Bd.App. 1975).

§ 4. The "Means" Clause

PAGE 48

[*Add new text after quoted matter ending with* "thereof.":]

A claim's element that is couched in terms of a "means plus function" statement must be interpreted, in compliance with 35 U.S.C. 112, as including all disclosed elements necessary to perform the stated function.[28.1] It is proper to look to the specification in interpreting claims reciting "means plus function," even if this results in a narrower interpretation of the claims than their broad "means plus function" clauses would at first indicate.[28.2]

28.1 General Electric Co. v. United States, 191 U.S.P.Q. 594 (Ct.Cl. 1976).

28.2 Lockheed Aircraft Corp. v. United States, 530 F.2d 956, 190 U.S.P.Q. 134, 145 (Ct.Cl. 1976).

Notes

PAGE 52

[*Add to footnote* **22**:]
Ex parte Schundehutte, 184 U.S.P.Q. 697 (P.O.Bd.App. 1973).

[*Add to footnote* **26**:]
In re Janakirama-Rao, 317 F.2d 951, 137 U.S.P.Q. 893 (C.C.P.A. 1963).

Chapter 4

SOME POPULARLY HELD MISCONCEPTIONS ABOUT PATENTS

§ 1. Patentability of Ideas

PAGE 56

[*Insert after first text paragraph:*]

More recently the Supreme Court has explicitly recognized that one may not patent an idea.[1.1] This position has been echoed by the Court of Customs & Patent Appeals.[1.2]

[1.1] Gottschalk v. Benson, 409 U.S. 63, 67, 175 U.S.P.Q. 673, 675 (1972).
[1.2] *In re* Christensen, 478 F.2d 1392, 1393-94, 178 U.S.P.Q. 35, 37 (C.C.P.A. 1973).

§ 4. "The Whole Must Equal the Sum of Its Parts"

PAGE 60

[*Add immediately before first full text paragraph:*]

The Court of Customs & Patent Appeals has on occasion employed the change-in-degree, change-in-kind dichotomy to distinguish the obvious from the non-obvious, respectively.[7.1]

[7.1] *In re* Waymouth, 499 F.2d 1273, 1276, 182 U.S.P.Q. 290, 293 (C.C.P.A. 1974).

§ 5. Patent Pending; Patent Medicine

PAGE 63

[*Add immediately before last text line on the page:*]

The controlling standard regarding false marking is not whether the patent incontrovertibly covers the marked article, but whether it reads on the article to the extent that a person could hold an honest belief that it applies.[21.1]

[21.1] United States ex rel. Scharmer v. Carrollton Mfg. Co., 377 F. Supp. 218, 220-21, 181 U.S.P.Q. 451, 452 (N.D. Ohio 1974).

Notes

PAGE 65

[*Add to footnote* **5**:]

Sakradia v. Ag Pro, Inc., 425 U.S. 273, 282, 189 U.S.P.Q. 449, 453, *rehearing denied* 426 U.S. 955 (1976); Anderson's-Black Rock v. Pavement Co., 396 U.S. 57, 61, 163 U.S.P.Q. 673, 674 (1969).

Chapter 5

STATUTORY SUBJECT MATTER

§ 1. Statutory Subject Matter

PAGE 73

[*Insert after text paragraph ending with footnote* **11**:]

The Court of Customs & Patent Appeals has said, however, that it does not subscribe to the broad proposition that process limitations can *never* serve to distinguish apparatus claims' subject matter from the prior art.[11.1] Regarding the relationship between a method and the apparatus used in carrying it out, the rule, at least in determining infringement, is that a method patent is not dependent on the form of the apparatus used. Infringement cannot usually be avoided merely by making slight innovations in the apparatus disclosed in the patent.

[11.1] *In re* Wertheim, 541 F.2d 257, 270, 191 U.S.P.Q. 90, 102 (C.C.P.A. 1976).
[11.2] CMI Corp. v. Metropolitan Enterprises, Inc., 534 F.2d 874, 881, 189 U.S.P.Q. 770, 776 (10th Cir. 1976).

§ 1[1]. Process

PAGE 74

[*In first complete text paragraph on the page, add after* "different process.[18]":]

Claims drawn to a machine and claims drawn to a method which can be performed by hand or by the use of a different machine represent two different inventions.[18.1]

[18.1] General Staple Co. v. Magnifica, 189 U.S.P.Q. 679, 687 (S.D.N.Y. 1976).

PAGE 75

[*In 10th text line on the page, delete all text after* "a physical result," *through end of the paragraph, and substitute:*]

method claims involving a computer program that effect a physical result have been held patentable by the Court of Customs & Patent

Appeals.[20.1] However, where the entire process is purely mental, such that all the steps are capable of being performed in one's head (as, for example, a technique for computing square roots), a process claim drawn to such subject matter is not deemed to fall within the purview of a statutory "process" as that term is used in Section 101.[21] Moreover, it can be argued that a patent on such a process would invade the freedom of thought, and so might violate the First Amendment. The result of such a purely mental process is not physical but rather consists merely of the production of numerical values. A computer program addressed to generating mere numerical values may, nevertheless, be patentable, if claimed as an apparatus, rather than as a process.[21.1] Thus, while a computer program couched as a process is deemed nonstatutory subject matter, a programmed computer claim (written in means-plus-function format) is regarded as a machine.[21.2] The rationale for this approach is that a computer with program A is a different apparatus from the same computer with program B.[21.3]

[20.1] *In re* Chatfield, — F.2d —, 191 U.S.P.Q. 730 (C.C.P.A. 1976).
[21] See Gottschalk v. Benson, 409 U.S. 63, 175 U.S.P.Q. 673 (1972).
[21.1] *In re* Noll, — F.2d —, 191 U.S.P.Q. 721 (C.C.P.A. 1976).
[21.2] *In re* Knowlton, 481 F.2d 1357, 178 U.S.P.Q. 486 and 618 (C.C.P.A. 1973).
[21.3] *In re* Comstock, 491 F.2d 905, 178 U.S.P.Q. 1973).

[*In penultimate line of text on the page, add after* "being old.":]

The materials employed in a process cannot be ignored in resolving the question of the patentability of process claims.[21.4]

[21.4] Ex parte Macy, 132 U.S.P.Q. 545 (P.O.Bd.App. 1960).

PAGE 76

[*In second text paragraph, add to text after sentence ending* "as a process.[25]":]

What about a "new use" or new application of an old *process*? While there is some authority to the contrary,[25.1] the better rule would seem to be that a new use for an old process or product is patentable if such new use or application satisfies the non-obviousness standard of Section 103.[25.2] A new use, if claimed as a process, is a new process.

[25.1] W.L. Gore & Associates, Inc. v. Carlisle Corp., 529 F.2d 614, 621, 189 U.S.P.Q. 129, 135 (3d Cir. 1976).

[25.2] Allegheny Drop Forge Co. v. Portec Inc., 541 F.2d 383, 386, 191 U.S.P.Q. 541, 543 (3d Cir. 1976).

[Add to text at end of § 1[1].]

Overruling what had been Patent Office practice, at least since *Ex parte Pointer*,[27.1] the Court of Customs & Patent Appeals held that an application may present both conventional product claims and product-by-process claims drawn to the same composition of matter.[27.2] It had been Patent Office practice to permit product-by-process claims only where an applicant alleged that the product could be defined in no other way. Under such practice, the presence of a conventional product claim precluded the inclusion of a product-by-process claim. The liberality of the Court of Customs & Patent Appeals on this point may not be shared by courts having jurisdiction over patent infringement. Thus, it has been held that claims defining a product by the process of making it are permissible only when that product cannot be otherwise defined.[27.3]

[27.1] 1891 C.D. 200, 570 O.G. 999 (Comm. Pat. 1891).

[27.2] *In re* Hughes, 496 F.2d 1216, 182 U.S.P.Q. 106 (C.C.P.A. 1974).

[27.3] Westwood Chemical, Inc. v. Dow Corning Corp., 189 U.S.P.Q. 649, 665 (E.D. Mich. 1975).

§ 1[5]. Designs

PAGE 79

[In sixth text line of this section, add after "utility or function.".]

The "utility requirement" of Section 101 is not applicable to design inventions and rejection of design claims for "lack of utility" is error.[39.1]

[39.1] *In re* Finch, 535 F.2d 70, 71, 190 U.S.P.Q. 64, 65 (C.C.P.A. 1976).

[In second line of third text paragraph, add after "new and unobvious.".]

The basic consideration in applying the unobviousness standard of Section 103 to a claimed design as a whole is the similarity of appearance between what is claimed and prior art designs. Though there may be differences in appearance between the claimed design and prior designs, the test remains whether the claimed design would have been obvious in view of such designs in the prior art.[44.1]

[44.1] *In re* Finch, 535 F.2d 70, 72, 190 U.S.P.Q. 64, 66 (C.C.P.A. 1976).

PAGE 80

[*In third full paragraph on the page, delete text after footnote* **54** *through end of the paragraph, and substitute:*]

There now is a standard filing fee ($20) for all design applications. The issue fee, however, varies according to the term elected. The choice of term is incorporated into the formal notice of allowance form.[54.1]

[54.1] M.P.E.P. 1505 (Rev.51, Jan. 1977).

[*Add to text at end of* § **1[5]**.]

The issue of infringement in design patent cases cannot be decided solely on an element-by-element or line-by-line comparison of the accused patented designs. The test of infringement in design patent cases may be stated as follows: If, in the eye of the ordinary observer giving such attention as a purchaser usually gives, the two designs are substantially the same and the resemblance is such as to deceive such an observer, inducing him to purchase one, supposing it to be the other, the patented design is infringed by the other. The "ordinary observer" is a hypothetical one, much the same as the "reasonable man" in negligence law. The test is an objective one. It must be applied by comparing the overall appearance of the two designs and not by selecting one or more features of which the observer particularly approves.[55.1]

[55.1] Summers v. Laubach, 191 U.S.P.Q. 114, 118 (D. Kan. 1974).

§ 1[6]. Plants

PAGE 81

[*In fourth text line, sentence ending in footnote* **57** *now reads:*]
Tuber propagated plants (such as potatoes) and plants found in an

uncultivated state are specifically excluded by statute from plant patent protection.[57]

[Add to text following sentence ending in footnote **57***:]*

Excluded by judicial construction are newly discovered bacteria.[57.1]

[57.1] *In re* Arzberger, 112 F.2d 834, 46 U.S.P.Q. 32 (C.C.P.A. 1940).

PAGE 82

[In sixth text line, add after "thereon.[67]"*:]*

Similarly, there is no requirement for a how-to-make disclosure in a plant patent application.[67.1]

[67.1] *In re* Greer, 484 F.2d 488, 179 U.S.P.Q. 301 (C.C.P.A. 1973).

§ 3. Multiple and Alternative Protection: Successive and Simultaneous

PAGE 84

[Insert the following text after third paragraph of this section:]

A design patent and a utility patent may well be issued on the same construction. However, each such patent must claim a separate, distinct patentable invention. In order to determine whether the same invention is claimed in design and utility patents, the picture claim of the design patent must be compared with the word claims of the utility patent. The mere use of the same design patent as the vehicle for describing the utility claimed in the utility patent is not dispositive. Impermissible double patenting exists if the feature in which the novel esthetic effect resides is the identical feature which produces the novel function so that a structure embodying the utility invention would of necessity embody the design, and vice versa. Cases which state that double patenting exists if the design claimed in the first-to-issue design patent cannot be employed without infringing the utility patent, and that double patent has not occurred if the second-to-issue utility patent encompasses designs other than identical subject matter if one of the claims being compared could be literally infringed without literally infringing the other, merely state corollaries to basic standard and can only be properly applied with reference to it. Double patenting in the design-utility situation cannot turn on niceties of precise ornamentation, but rather must turn on the presence or absence of design features which produce the novel function claimed in the utility patent. If narrow decorative variations which contribute in no way to the novel function were allowed to enter the inquiry, it would become virtually impossible ever to find double patenting in the design-utility situation.[80.1]

[80.1] Ropat Corp. v. McGraw-Edison Co., 535 F.2d 378, 382, 191 U.S.P.Q. 556, 558-59 (7th Cir. 1976).

Notes

PAGE 86

[*Add to footnote* 13:]

Gross v. General Motors Corp., 390 F. Supp. 236, 185 U.S.P.Q. 262 (D.Mass), *aff'd* 521 F.2d 45, 186 U.S.P.Q. 433 (1st Cir. 1975).

Example of a claim held invalid under 35 U.S.C. 101 as an attempt to patent compressability, a natural property of gases:

1. A pneumatic yieldable load-bearing device comprising an enclosed container having wallportions movable and effective to vary the volume of the container, said portions supporting a load tending to move said portions, and a gas within said container, said gas being under a pressure effective to support said load and having a ratio of Cp/Cv of no more than about 1.25 and being uncondensable at temperatures and pressures within the container encountered during normal operation of the device.

[*Add to footnote* 26:]

Pfizer, Inc. v. International Rectifier Corp., 538 F.2d 180, 188, 190 U.S.P.Q. 273, 280 (8th Cir. 1976), citing PATENT LAW FUNDAMENTALS as authority.

[*Add to footnote* 27:]

In re Wertheim, 541 F.2d 257, 271, 191 U.S.P.Q. 90, 103 (C.C.P.A. 1976); *In re* Hirao, 535 F.2d 67, 69, 190 U.S.P.Q. 15, 17 (C.C.P.A. 1976).

[*Add to footnote* 33:]

Funk Bros. Seed Co. v. Kalo, 333 U.S. 127, 130, 76 U.S.P.Q. 280, 281 (1948).

PAGE 88

[*Add to footnote* 80:]

Anchor Hocking Corp. v. Eyelet Specialty Co., 377 F. Supp. 98, 183 U.S.P.Q. 87 (D.Del. 1974); Mr. Hanger, Inc. v. Cut Rate Plastic Hangers, Inc., 372 F. Supp. 88, 181 U.S.P.Q. 850 (E.D.N.Y. 1974).

[*Add to footnote* **89**:]

In re Soccer Sport Supply Co., 507 F.2d 1400, 184 U.S.P.Q. 345 (C.C.P.A. 1975); *In re* Honeywell, 497 F.2d 1344, 181 U.S.P.Q. 821 (C.C.P.A. 1974), *cert. denied* 419 U.S. 1080 (1974).

Chapter 6

NOVELTY

§ 1. The Prior Art

PAGE 91

[*Add new text after last line on the page:*]

Thus, the mere discovery of an end use (as abrasive articles) for a composition of matter which in the prior art was used only as an intermediate (in the production of abrasive articles) does not entitle the discoverer of that end use to a patent on the composition.[1.1]

[1.1] *In re* Mullin, 481 F.2d 1333, 179 U.S.P.Q. 97 (C.C.P.A. 1973).

§ 2. The Doctrine of Inherency

PAGE 93

[*Add immediately preceding first text paragraph:*]

In order for something to be "inherent" in a disclosure it must be the necessary and only reasonable construction to be given to the disclosure, that is, the result claimed must inevitably occur.[3.1] A patent claiming a process inherently performed by old apparatus, and old product inherently produced, is invalid for want of novelty.[3.2]

[3.1] Westwood Chemical, Inc. v. Dow Corning Corp., 189 U.S.P.Q. 649, 678-79 (E.D.Mich. 1975).
[3.2] Grain Products, Inc. v. Lincoln Grain, Inc., 191 U.S.P.Q. 177 (S.D.Ind. 1976).

§ 3. Novelty and Anticipation

PAGE 94

[*Insert immediately preceding last text line on the page:*]

An accidental and unappreciated duplication of an invention does not defeat the patent right of one who, though later in time, was the first to recognize that which constitutes the inventive subject matter.[7.1] An accidental or unwitting duplication of an invention

17

cannot constitute an anticipation.[7.2] A structure that was altered to meet a customer's specifications, then abandoned and thereafter never published or otherwise developed, compels its elimination from consideration as a branch of prior art.[7.3] Similarly, an unexplained, misdesignated representation was deemed not to be effective prior art.[7.4] Nor is an abandoned experiment effective prior art.[7.5]

[7.1] Eibel Process Co. v. Minnesota & Ontario Paper Co., 261 U.S. 45, 66 (1923); The General Tire & Rubber Co. v. Jefferson Chemical Co., 497 F.2d 1283, 1291, 182 U.S.P.Q. 70, 76 (2d Cir. 1974), rev'g 180 U.S.P.Q. 33 (S.D.N.Y. 1973), cert. denied 419 U.S. 968 (1974); Silvestri v. Grant, 496 F.2d 593, 597, 181 U.S.P.Q. 706, 708 (C.C.P.A. 1974), cert. denied 420 U.S. 928 (1975).

[7.2] In re Felton, 484 F.2d 495, 500, 179 U.S.P.Q. 295, 298 (C.C.P.A. 1973).

[7.3] Cathodic Protection Service v. American Smelting & Refining Co., 190 U.S.P.Q. 254, 264 (S.D.Tex. 1975).

[7.4] Columbia Broadcasting System, Inc. v. Zenith Radio Corp., 391 F. Supp. 780, 788, 185 U.S.P.Q. 662, 668 (N.D.Ill. 1975).

[7.5] Mobil Oil Corp. v. W.R. Grace & Co., 367 F. Supp. 207, 255, 180 U.S.P.Q. 418, 451 (D.Conn. 1973).

PAGE 95

[*In first text paragraph, add after sentence ending in footnote* **8:**]

An inventor is assumed to have full and comprehensive knowledge of the prior art, in legal contemplation.[8.1] Moreover, everything disclosed in patent is deemed prior art, regardless of its validity.[8.2]

[8.1] Allegheny Drop Forge Co. v. Portec Inc., 541 F.2d 383, 384, 191 U.S.P.Q. 541, 542 (3d Cir. 1976); Ex parte Varga, 189 U.S.P.Q. 204, 208 (P.O.Bd.App. 1973).

[8.2] Turzillo v. P & Z Mergentine, 532 F.2d 1393, 1402, 189 U.S.P.Q. 783, 790 (D.C.C. 1976).

[*Insert after first full text paragraph on the page:*]

To constitute an anticipation, all the claimed elements must be found in exactly the same situation and united in the same way to perform the identical function in a single prior art reference.[9.1] Uncorroborated oral testimony by a witness speaking only from memory in regard to past transactions, in the absence of contemporaneous documentary or physical evidence, is insufficient to show anticipation of an issued patent.[9.2] However, an applicant's designation of a figure in his application as "prior art" has been deemed an admission that such was the case.[9.3]

[9.1] Tights v. Acme-McCrary Corp., 541 F.2d 1047, 1056, 191 U.S.P.Q. 305, 310 (4th Cir. 1976). See also, *In re* Outtrup, 531 F.2d 1055, 1058, 189 U.S.P.Q. 345, 347 (C.C.P.A. 1976).

[9.2] Lockheed Aircraft Corp. v. United States, 190 U.S.P.Q. 134, 140 (Ct.Cl. 1976). See also, Carter v. Rice, 398 F. Supp. 474, 476, 188 U.S.P.Q. 451, 453, (N.D.Tex. 1975).

[9.3] *In re* Nomiya, 509 F.2d 566, 570-71, 184 U.S.P.Q. 607, 611-12 (C.C.P.A. 1975).

§ 4. Patents and Printed Publications

PAGE 96

[Insert after first text paragraph:]

This is the case with the West German Gebrauchsmuster, or utility model, which is a public record in the German Patent Office that serves to charge practitioners in the art with notice of what it discloses.[9.4]

[9.4] Allegheny Drop Forge Co. v. Portec, Inc., 541 F.2d 383, 385, 191 U.S.P.Q. 541, 542 (3d Cir. 1976).

[Add after last sentence on the page:]

Accordingly, abandoned patent applications which are not open to public scrutiny are not prior art.[13.1]

The remoteness of the distribution of the printed publication from the United States and the limited geographic extent of the distribution are immaterial. All that is required is that the document be printed and so disseminated as to provide wide access to some segment of the public. The key factor is not access by a specific segment of the public, or number of persons, or even by any specific means, but simply distribution to any segment of the public. The distribution of 500 instructional booklets and thousands of advertisements, though only in Japan, rendered a disclosure a printed publication within the contemplation of Section 102(a).[13.2] An IBM Technical Bulletin deposited only in the Patent Office Library, the New York Public Library and the Brown University Library was deemed a "printed publication."[13.3] Even more startling was the holding that a single copy transmitted to a professional society for possible presentation, that was merely referred to the society's editorial board and never presented, was a "printed publication."[13.4]

[13.1] Sears v. Gottschalk, 502 F.2d 122, 128-29, 183 U.S.P.Q. 134, 137-38 (4th Cir. 1974), *cert. denied* 420 U.S. 921 (1976).

13.2 Popeil Bros., Inc. v. Schick Electric, Inc., 494 F.2d 162, 166, 181 U.S.P.Q. 482, 485 (7th Cir. 1974).

13.3 Potter Instrument Co. v ODEC Computer Systems, Inc., 370 F. Supp. 198, 181 U.S.P.Q. 572, 581 (D.R.I. 1974).

13.4 Maurice A. Garbill, Inc. v. Boeing Col, 385 F. Supp. 1, 41, 180 U.S.P.Q. 294, 302 (C.D.Cal. 1973).

§ 7. Experimental Use

PAGE 100

[Add immediately preceding first full text paragraph:]

Obviously there can be a "public use" or a placing "on sale" only after there is an invention, that is, only after there has been a reduction to practice. Courts are divided on whether a use can be "experimental" after there has been a reduction to practice. The Seventh Circuit has held that a use cannot be deemed experimental after a reduction to practice has occurred.[23.1] Whether a prior use by the inventor was "experimental" or "public" is a question of fact which precludes summary judgment.[23.2]

23.1 *In re* Yarn Processing Patent Validity Litigation, 498 F.2d 271, 277-78, 183 U.S.P.Q. 65, 71 (5th Cir. 1974), *rev'g summary judgment on other grounds* 360 F. Supp. 74, 182 U.S.P.Q. 323 (S.D.Fla. 1974).

23.2 Finney v. United States, 178 U.S.P.Q. 235, 238 (Ct.Cl. 1973).

[In eighth line of first full text paragraph, add before "On the other hand":]

However, it has been held in the Ninth Circuit that a sale or an offering for sale precludes any inquiry into the experimental nature of the sale *unless* the contract of sale or the offering for sale contains an express or clearly implied condition that the sale or offering is made primarily for experimental use. Even under this rule, a sale or offering would not of itself invalidate the patent, nor would it preclude further inquiry into the experimental nature of the use where the contract or offer (1) stated that the sale was for experimental purposes; or (2) showed that the device was still experimental and that no workable prototype had been made; or (3) required that the invention be kept confidential or from public view, or that reports on the use of the invention should be supplied to the inventor; or (4) other similar statements appeared from which it could clearly be implied that the sale or the offering was made for an experimental purpose.[25.1]

An offer to make a product, accompanied by a hand-made sample eighteen months before the application was filed and contemporaneous letters showing that both the product and offer were experimental, was held not to have constituted a placing of the invention "on sale."[25.2]

[25.1] Robbins Co. v. Laurence Mfg. Co., 482 F.2d 426, 434, 178 U.S.P.Q. 577, 582 (9th Cir. 1973), *cert. denied* 414 U.S. 874 (1974).
[25.2] A.D.M. Corp. v. Spud Master Packaging Corp., 183 U.S.P.Q. 769 (D.N.J. 1974).

[Insert between first and second full text paragraphs:]

A single public use or sale may trigger the running of the time limit for filing a patent application.[27.1] Use of a device under conditions of limited public access (as a sterile operation room) may nonetheless result in a holding of public use or "on sale."[27.2] The sale of the product of a process constitutes a public use of the process.[27.3]

[27.1] Kastar, Inc. v. K Mart Enterprises, Inc., 190 U.S.P.Q. 550, 553 (E.D.N.Y. 1976).
[27.2] Marrese v. Richard's Medical Equipment, Inc., 504 F.2d 479, 482, 183 U.S.P.Q. 517, 519 (7th Cir. 1974).
[27.3] Kalvar Corp. v. Xidex Corp., 384 F. Supp. 1126, 1136, 182 U.S.P.Q. 532, 537 (N.D.Cal. 1973).

[Insert between second and third full text paragraphs:]

Testing of the marketability may constitute an experimental use under the appropriate circumstances.[28.1]

[28.1] Interlego A.G. v. F.A.O. Schwarz, Inc., 191 U.S.P.Q. 129 (N.D.Ga. 1976).

[Insert immediately preceding last text paragraph on the page:]

While a complete transaction is not necessary to prove that an invention was "on sale," it must be established not only that the inventor engaged in conduct which might be characterized as selling activity, but also that the invention existed as a complete article of sale such as to create an opportunity for present public use.[33.1] Similarly, a contract to build a machine in the future was deemed not to have placed the machine "on sale."[33.2] The fact that only part of the patented device was on hand at the time of the alleged "on sale" precluded a finding of "on sale."[33.3]

[33.1] Trans-World Display Corp. v. Mechtronics, Inc., 182 U.S.P.Q. 469, 470 (S.D.N.Y. 1974).

[33.2] Orton v. Robinson Corp., 378 F. Supp. 930, 183 U.S.P.Q. 477 (W.D.Pa. 1974).

[33.3] C.T.S. Corp. v. Piher International Corp., 184 U.S.P.Q. 399 (N.D.Ill. 1974).

[Add after last line of text on the page:]

The experimental use exception to a public use benefits only the inventor, and an experimental public use by a third party, even though not fully successful, is a public use as to the rest of the world.[34.1] Thus, several unrestricted offerings for sale of sample quantities of a plastic to customers for their experimental use amounted to an "on sale."[34.2]

The burden of establishing that a patented product was "on sale" before the critical date is on the person asserting the same and it must be established by clear and convincing evidence. Invalidity may be established either by showing non-secret use of the invention prior to the critical date or by establishing that the inventor has commercially exploited the invention prior to the critical date without injunction or secrecy.[34.3]

[34.1] Dunlop Co. v. Kelsey-Hayes, 484 F.2d 407, 413, 179 U.S.P.Q. 129, 133 (6th Cir. 1973), *cert. denied* 415 U.S. 917 (1974); Bird Provision Co. v. Owens County Sausage, Inc., 379 F. Supp. 744, 747, 184 U.S.P.Q. 174, 176 (N.D.Tex. 1974).

[34.2] Dart Industries, Inc. v. E.I. duPont & Co., 489 F.2d 1359, 179 U.S.P.Q. 392 (7th Cir. 1973), *cert denied* 417 U.S. 933 (1973), *rev'd* 348 F. Supp. 1338, 175 U.S.P.Q. 540 (N.D. Ill. 1972).

[34.3] The Red Cross Manufacturing Corp. v. Toro Sales Co., 525 F.2d 1135, 188 U.S.P.Q. 241 (7th Cir. 1975).

§ 8.   Doctrine of Late Claiming

PAGE 102

[Add to text at end of the section:]

Some courts have gone beyond this, holding that any claim presented to the Patent Office more than a year after that which such claim reads on has gone into public use is invalid—wherever such late claim differs materially in scope from any claim not presented in the application as originally filed, even where the late claim was fully supported by the disclosure as originally filed. These courts deem the intervening rights of the public as paramount to those of the patentee.[37.1]

Most courts, however, take the position that the doctrine of late claiming can apply only where the specification as originally filed has somehow been altered and such alteration is relied upon to support a later introduced claim. It is immaterial whether the alteration is made in an amendment or in a reissue application.[37.2]

[37.1] Kahn v. Dynamics Corp., 367 F. Supp. 63, 180 U.S.P.Q. 247 (S.D.N.Y.·1975), aff'd 508 F. 2d 939, 184 U.S.P.Q. 260 (2d Cir. 1975); Wayne-Gossard Corp. v. Moretz Hosiery Mills, Inc., 539 F.2d 986, 191 U.S.P.Q. 543 (4th Cir. 1976).

[37.2] Cardinal of Adrian, Inc. v. Peerless Wood Products, Inc., 515 F.2d 534, 185 U.S.P.Q. 712 (6th Cir. 1975); Price v. Lake Sales Supply R.M., Inc., 510 F.2d 388, 183 U.S.P.Q. 519 (10th Cir. 1974); St. Regis Paper v. Bemis Co., Inc., 403 F. Supp. 776, 188 U.S.P.Q. 107 (S.D.Ill. 1975); Potter Instrument Co. v. Bucode, Inc., 184 U.S.P.Q. 662 (E.D.N.Y. 1975).

§ 9. Abandonment

PAGE 103

[Add after first full text paragraph:]

A distinction has also been drawn between forfeiture and abandonment: A person forfeits the right to a patent because of *designed* delay in filing for a patent while abandonment contemplates a deliberate, although not necessarily an express, surrender of any right to a patent. The purposeful, unwarranted delay in seeking a patent necessary for a holding of forfeiture can occur only after the inventor possesses an invention capable of patenting.[42.1]

[42.1] *In re* Yarn Processing Patent Validity Litigation, 401 F.Supp. 673, 677, 189 U.S.P.Q. 598, 602 (S.D.Fla. 1975).

PAGE 104

[Insert between first and second full text paragraphs:]

While there are cases in which the character of the commercial exploitation of an invention will be relevant to the issue of abandonment, the prompt filing of a patent application and its diligent prosecution foreclose the contention that the invention was abandoned within the meaning of Section 102(c), even though a decision was made to postpone commercial development.[46.1] Abandonment is primarily an issue of fact, dependent on the inventor's intent.[46.2] The concept of abandonment contemplates a voluntary decision by the original inventor to terminate any effort to practice his conception.[46.3]

An eight-year delay between actual reduction to practice and filing a patent application was "unreasonable as a matter of law."[46.4] A lapse of six years between the time of actual reduction to practice and the filing of a patent application was deemed to constitute a prima facie case of abandonment.[46.5] A two-year delay in filing a patent application was not deemed an abandonment, where during the interim the applicant had sought FDA registration.[46.6] Similarly, a two-year delay in filing attributable to a busy patent attorney's backlog was not deemed an abandonment.[46.7] A lapse of over one and one-half years between dismantling of a physical embodiment of the invention and patent committee meeting at which a decision was made to file a patent application was deemed not evidence of an intent to abandon the invention. That the inventor was assigned the task of drafting the patent disclosure was taken as an implication that invention was not truly abandoned.[46.8]

[46.1] CTS Corp. v. Piher International Corp., 527 F.2d 95, 106, 188 U.S.P.Q. 419, 428 (7th Cir. 1975).

[46.2] General Foods Corp. v. Unarco Industries, Inc., 188 U.S.P.Q. 500, 502 (N.D.Ill. 1975).

[46.3] Allen v. W.H. Brady Co., 508 F.2d 64, 67, 184 U.S.P.Q. 385, 386 (7th Cir. 1975).

[46.4] Adler v. Hair, 188 U.S.P.Q. 186, 189 (Bd.Pat.Int. 1975).

[46.5] Aplan v. Aubrey, 180 U.S.P.Q. 529 (Bd.Pat.Int. 1973).

[46.6] Silvestri v. Grant, 496 F.2d 593, 601-602, 181 U.S.P.Q. 706, 711 (C.C.P.A. 1974).

[46.7] Blicharz v. Hays, 496 F.2d 603, 608, 181 U.S.P.Q. 712, 716 (C.C.P.A. 1974).

[46.8] Cochran v. Kresock, 530 F.2d 385, 392, 188 U.S.P.Q. 553, 558 (C.C.P.A. 1976).

[*In sixth line of second full text paragraph, add after* "States.":]

, but (3) only where the inventorship entity of the foreign patent is identical with the inventorship entity that made application in the United States, or is the legal representative or assignee thereof.[46.9]

[46.9] Ex parte Meunier, 188 U.S.P.Q. 532, 533 (P.O.Bd.App. 1974).

[*Add after last text paragraph on the page:*]

The bar of "patented under 35 U.S.C. 102(d)" applies when the right to exclude others begins, even though suit to enforce such right may not begin until a later date. In Japan and Great Britain the date which begins the right to exclude coincides with the date of publication, though the right to institute infringement proceedings does not begin until the day on which the patent is sealed.[46.10] A West German *Offenlegungsschrift* does not constitute "patented" within the meaning of Section 102(d), as the right to enforce the grant is subject to a condition precedent of a later *Auslegeschrift*.[46.11] The delivre (delivery) date of a French patent, that is, the day on which a decree of issuance is signed by the French Patent Office, is the effective date on which an invention is "patented" in France within the meaning of Section 102(d).[46.12]

[46.10] Ex parte Iizuka, 171 U.S.P.Q. — (P.O.Bd.App. 1970).

[46.11] Ex parte Links, 184 U.S.P.Q. 429 (P.O.Bd.App. 1975).

[46.12] The Duplan Corp. v. Deering Milliken Research Corp., 540 F.2d 1215, 179 U.S.P.Q. 449 (4th Cir. 1973).

PAGE 105

[Insert between first and second text paragraphs:]

Section 102(e) is an exception to the general rule that prior art knowledge must be public in order to defeat another's patent rights. A Defensive Publication is not a patent and therefore does not fall within the exception provided by Section 102(e). A Defensive Publication is no more than a publication and so cannot defeat another's right to a patent prior to its actual publication date. The application forming the basis of a Defensive Publication is not available to the public until the date of publication of the abstract of the Defensive Publication. Alien Property Custodian publications are effective as references only as of their publication dates.[47.1]

Section 102(g) negates novelty where the same invention was made earlier by another inventorship entity in the United States and such earlier inventorship entity is deemed not to have abandoned, suppressed, or concealed the invention. Section 102(g) does not require that there have been any public knowledge of the earlier invention. Section 102(g) is the basis for (1) an inter partes proceeding, known as an interference, to determine priority of invention; it may also form the basis of (2) a defense in a suit for patent infringement. Recently, Section 102(g) has been applied in (3) ex parte patent prosecution in the following manner. The Patent Office rejected an applicant for patent on the basis of an earlier filed U.S. patent specification as prior art. While the filing date of the patent specification relied upon as prior art was earlier than the applicant's U.S. filing date the applicant proffered an affidavit under Rule 131 to antedate the patent specification as a prior art reference. The position of the

Patent Office, which was upheld by the Court of Customs & Patent Appeals, was that though the affidavit had overcome the patent reference as prior art under Section 102(e) it was insufficient to overcome the patent reference under Section 102(g), as the invention disclosed in the patent specification must have been made at a point in time prior to its filing date.[47.2]

6/1/75	6/1/75	6/2/75	2/1/76
U.S. Patent's date of invention 102(s) critical date	Applicant's date of invention	U.S. Patent Reference's application date	Applicant's U.S. filing date

Another interesting, if not anomalous, result created by Section 102(g) involved the following facts. In an infringement suit it was established that application for the patented invention had been made by another (A) prior to the patentee's filing date. Such earlier applicant had abandoned his application as a result of an adverse ruling in an interference proceeding while the patentee's application was pending before the Patent Office. The prevailing party in that interference had neither described nor claimed the precise invention claimed in the abandoned application and the patent in suit, but rather an invention generic to it. The patent was held invalid under Section 102(g) in that before the applicant's invention the invention was made by another who had not abandoned, suppressed, or concealed it. While the court's decision was based at least in part on the fact that the winning party to the interference must have learned of the invention contained in the now abandoned application, and as the prevailing party in the interference he was the successor to that invention, perhaps if the patentee's application had been filed later than it actually was—late enough so that the prior application had already gone abandoned—the patent would not have been held invalid under Section 102(g).[47.3]

A	Patentee	A	Patent
Filed	Filed	Abandoned	Issued

As a defense to an interference suit, the accused infringer argued that the patent was invalid under Section 102(g) because application had been made earlier in the name of three inventors, and subsequently abandoned, but not until after the application which matured into the patent in suit was filed in the name of those three inventors plus two additional inventors. The patentee's position was that the later application had been filed to correct an error in the inventorship entity. The court held that the three original applicants were not "another" within the meaning of Section 102(g).[47.4]

Under Section 102(g) prior invention by another will not defeat the right to a patent of a subsequent inventor where the prior inventor has either abandoned, suppressed or concealed his invention. There seems to be a divergence in views on the effect of commercial exploitation on suppression and concealment. The Court of Customs & Patent Appeals has taken the position that a finding of suppression or concealment is not negated merely because a secret use of the invention is commercial. As the Court of Customs & Patent Appeals sees it, what is determinative is whether the public has gained knowledge of the invention such that its preservation in the public domain is assured.[47.5] Each case involving the issue of suppression or concealment, in the opinion of the Court of Customs & Patent Appeals, must be considered on its own particular set of facts. In such consideration two guide posts have been firmly established:

First—The length of time from actual reduction to practice to filing of an application for a patent is not determinative. Mere delay, without more, is not sufficient to establish suppression or concealment. However, one who delays filing his application does so at the peril of a finding of suppression or concealment due to the circumstances surrounding the delay.

Second—The spurring into filing an application for a patent by knowledge of another's entry into the field (for example, by the issuance of a patent) is not essential to a finding of suppression or concealment.

Accordingly, a suppression of invention, within the meaning of Section 102(g) was found where the junior party delayed filing a patent application for 27 months after reducing his invention to practice, despite the continuous demand for the invention.[47.6]

The Seventh Circuit Court of Appeals, however, has taken the position that public use of an invention forecloses a conclusion of suppression even though the public use does not disclose how to practice the invention, since use gives the public the benefit of the invention.[47.7]

Suppression and concealment will not be presumed by mere lapse of time.[47.8] A two-year hiatus between actual reduction to practice and patent application filing date was deemed sufficient to create an *inference* of abandonment, suppression, and concealment, where filing date of adverse interference party intervened.[47.9]

47.1 Ex parte Osmond, 191 U.S.P.Q. 334 (P.O.Bd.App. 1976). See also Ex parte Osmond, 191 U.S.P.Q. 340 (P.O.Bd.App. 1976).

47.2 See *In re* Bass, 474 F.2d 1276, 177 U.S.P.Q. 178 (C.C.P.A. 1973); *In re* Hellsund, 474 F.2d 1307, 177 U.S.P.Q. 170 (C.C.P.A. 1973).

47.3 Allen v. W.H. Brady Co., 508 F.2d 64, 184 U.S.P.Q. 385 (7th Cir. 1974).

47.4 General Foods Corp. v. Unarco Industries, Inc. 188 U.S.P.Q. 500 (N.D.Ill. 1975).

47.5 Palmer v. Dudzik, 481 F.2d 1377, 1387, 178 U.S.P.Q. 608, 615-16 (C.C.P.A. 1973).

47.6 Young v. Dworkin, 489 F.2d 1277, 1280-81, 180 U.S.P.Q. 388, 392 (C.C.P.A. 1974).

47.7 Dunlop Holding Ltd. v. Ram Golf Corp., 524 F.2d 33, 37, 188 U.S.P.Q. 481, 484 (7th Cir. 1975), *cert. denied* 424 U.S. 958 (1976).

47.8 Myers v. Feigelman, 190 U.S.P.Q. 198 (Bd.Pat.Int. 1973).

47.9 Vancil v. Arata, 191 U.S.P.Q. 464, 465 (Bd.Pat.Int. 1976).

Notes

PAGE 106

[*Add to footnote* 1:]

Clopay Corp. v. Blessings Corp., 422 F. Supp. 1312, 1317, 191 U.S.P.Q. 751, 755 (D.Del. 1976), citing PATENT LAW FUNDAMENTALS as authority.

[*Add to footnote* 5:]

In re Herz, 537 F.2d 549, 551, 190 U.S.P.Q. 461, 463 (C.C.P.A. 1976); *In re* Mott, 539 F.2d 1291, 1296, 190 U.S.P.Q. 536, 541 (C.C.P.A. 1976); *In re* Saether, 492 F.2d 849, 181 U.S.P.Q. 36, 39 (C.C.P.A. 1974).

[*Add to footnote* 9:]

Dunlop Holdings Ltd. v. Ram Golf Corp., 524 F.2d 33, 188 U.S.P.Q. 481 (7th Cir. 1975), *cert. denied* 424 U.S. 958 (1976).

[*Add to footnote* 35:]

Faulkner v. Baldwin Piano & Organ Co., 189 U.S.P.Q. 695, 723 (N.D.Ill. 1976).

Chapter 7

UTILITY

PAGE 109

[*Add after the last text line on the page:*]

Although the utility requirement of Section 112 has sometimes been characterized as the "how-to-use requirement," the Court of Customs & Patent Appeals has stated that Section 112 does *not* require the specification to describe how to use the invention but rather merely *to enable any person skilled in the art to which it pertains, or with which it is most nearly connected, to . . . use* the invention. Thus, in evaluating whether there has been compliance with the utility requirement of Section 112, what those skilled in the relevant art already knew or were presumed to have known from the disclosures available to them before the filing date of the specification under consideration must be evaluated.[a1]

[a1] *In re* Irani, 487 F.2d 924, 925, 180 U.S.P.Q. 44, 45 (C.C.P.A. 1973).

PAGE 110

[*Insert immediately preceding last text paragraph on the page (paragraph running over to page 111):*]

Inoperativeness is not established merely by showing that a particular disclosed embodiment for carrying out the principles of the invention is lacking in perfection.[1.1]

[1.1] Decca Ltd. v. United States, 188 U.S.P.Q. 167, 170 (Ct.Cl. 1975).

[*In sixth text line of last paragraph on the page (paragraph running over to page 111), add after "patent therefor.²":*]

All embodiments within a claim's scope need not be equally effective to be entitled to patent protection.[2.1]

[2.1] *In re* Fouche, 439 F.2d 1237, 169 U.S.P.Q. 429 (C.C.P.A. 1971); Ex parte Gastambide, 189 U.S.P.Q. 643 (P.O.Bd.App. 1974).

PAGE 111

[*Insert between fifth and sixth full text paragraphs:*]

This rule also applies to compositions of matter. Thus, where it was alleged in the specification that a composition was useful as a drug for treating arthritis in certain animals and possibly also in treating humans for the same ailment, proof that the composition was efficacious as a drug for treating arthritis in the animal species alluded to in the specification was deemed sufficient to satisfy the utility requirement of Section 101.[7.1] The invalidity for lack of utility of some of the claims of a patent does not render the remaining claims unenforceable where the claims were made in good faith.[7.2]

[7.1] *In re* Malachowski, 530 F.2d 1402, 189 U.S.P.Q. 432 (C.C.P.A. 1976).
[7.2] CPC International, Inc. v. Standard Brands Inc., 184 U.S.P.Q. 332 (D.Del. 1974).

PAGE 112

[*In sixth text line on the page, add after* "utility requirement.":]

However, the mere discovery of an end use (as abrasive articles) for a composition of matter which in the prior art was used only as an intermediate (in the production of abrasive articles) does not entitle the discoverer of that end use to a patent on the composition.[10.1]

[10.1] *In re* Mullin, 481 F.2d 1333, 179 U.S.P.Q. 97 (C.C.P.A. 1973).

[*In 12th text line, add after* "possess inertia.":]

The Court of Customs & Patent Appeals sustained a finding of utility by the Board of Appeals adequate to support an interference count to: "Crystalline microspheres consisting essentially of uranium mononitride having a density of at least 90% of theoretical," based solely upon publications indicating that a number of installations had been studying uranium mononitride as a nuclear fuel with promising results. Apparently the publication relied upon said nothing about uranium mononitride in the form of crystalline microspheres.[10.2]

[10.2] Trigiana v. Jens, 482 F.2d 1381, 179 U.S.P.Q. 236 (C.C.P.A. 1973).

[Insert after second full text paragraph on the page:]

Where the Patent Office alleges that the stated utility is of such an unpredictable nature that one could not be certain that all animals and compounds within the scope of the claims would react in the stated manner, it is incumbent upon the Patent Office to explain why it doubts the truth or accuracy of any statement in applicant's disclosure and to back up assertions of its own with acceptable evidence or reasoning which is inconsistent with the contested statement.[13.1]

It is not proper for the Patent Office to require clinical testing in humans to rebut a prima facie case for lack of utility when the pertinent references which establish the prima facie case show in vitro tests and when they do not show in vivo tests employing standard experimental animals.[13.2]

[13.1] Ex parte Kenaga, 190 U.S.P.Q. 346, 347 (P.O.Bd.App. 1975).
[13.2] *In re* Langer, 503 F.2d 1380, 1393, 183 U.S.P.Q. 288, 297 (C.C.P.A. 1974).

Notes

PAGE 114

[Add to footnote 9:]

Anderson v. Natta, 480 F.2d 1392, 1395, 178 U.S.P.Q. 458, 460 (C.C.P.A. 1973).

Chapter 8

NONOBVIOUSNESS

PAGE 117

[In fourth line of first full text paragraph, add after "one another.":]

   Lack of novelty has been characterized as the epitome of obviousness.[1.1]

[1.1] *In re* Wertheim, 541 F.2d 257, 271, 191 U.S.P.Q. 90, 104 (C.C.P.A. 1976); *In re* Pearson, 494 F.2d 1399, 1402, 181 U.S.P.Q. 641, 644 (C.C.P.A. 1974); *In re* Kalm, 378 F.2d 959, 962, 154 U.S.P.Q. 10, 12 (C.C.P.A. 1967).

[Insert immediately before last text paragraph on the page (paragraph running over to page 118):]

   Patentable ingenuity may, and often does, reside in perception of a desirable goal which, once perceived, is achievable through the exercise of routine skill.[7.1] Moreoever, simplicity should not be confused with obviousness. In fact, simplicity does not in itself detract from inventiveness.[7.2] Simplicity—particularly in an old and crowded art—may argue for patentability, rather than against it.[7.3]

[7.1] Lerner v. Child Guidance Products, Inc., 406 F. Supp. 560, 565, 189 U.S.P.Q. 83, 88 (S.D.N.Y. 1975).

[7.2] Saf-Gard Products, Inc. v. Service Parts, Inc., 532 F.2d 1266, 1272, 190 U.S.P.Q. 455, 460 (9th Cir. 1976).

[7.3] *In re* Meng, 492 F.2d 843, 848, 181 U.S.P.Q. 94, 97 (C.C.P.A. 1974).

---

§ 2. The Nonobviousness Standard of Section 103

PAGE 120

[Insert new text following paragraph ending in footnote 21:]

   That a startling discovery resulted from doing what was said to be stupid has been taken as evidence of nonobviousness.[21.1]

[21.1] Ortho Pharmaceutical Corp. v. American Hospital Supply Corp., 534 F.2d 89, 93, 190 U.S.P.Q. 397, 400 (7th Cir. 1976).

PAGE 121

[*Insert text immediately preceding last paragraph on the page (paragraph running over to page 122):*]

While the question of obviousness is one of law, its resolution requires several antecedent factual determinations, including: (1) prior art's scope and content; (2) differences between prior art and claims; (3) level of ordinary skill in the art.[28.1] Since the ultimate question of obviousness is a matter of law, the "clearly erroneous" standard of review of Fed.R.Civ.P. 52(a) does not apply.[28.2]

[28.1] Parker v. Motorola, Inc., 524 F.2d 518, 531, 188 U.S.P.Q. 225, 235 (5th Cir. 1975), *cert. denied* 427 U.S. 908 (1976). See also, Moore v. Schultz, 491 F.2d 294, 300, 180 U.S.P.Q. 548, 552 (10th Cir. 1974).

[28.2] Airlite Plastics Co. v. Plastitite Corp., 526 F.2d 1078, 1080, 189 U.S.P.Q. 327, 328 (8th Cir. 1975).

[*In last text line on the page, add after "insurmountable.*[31]*":*]

Obviousness is measured by what would have been obvious to one reasonably skilled in the applicable art rather than what would be obvious to the layman.[31.1]

It has been held that the trial judge cannot be equated with "a person having ordinary skill in the art."[31.2] Numerous judges have recognized the shortcoming of requiring judges whose knowledge of the relevant technology derives primarily or even solely from the explanation of counsel to pass upon patent cases.[31.3] Recently this practice has been characterized as an "absurdity."[31.4]

[31.1] Dann v. Johnston, 425 U.S. 219, 229, 189 U.S.P.Q. 257, 261 (1976).

[31.2] Buzzelli v. Minnesota Mining & Mfg. Co., 480 F.2d 541, 542-43, 178 U.S.P.Q. 260, 261 (6th Cir. 1973).

[31.3] Parke-Davis v. H.K. Mulford Co., 189 F. 95, 115 (2d Cir. 1911) (L. Hand, J.); Picard v. United Aircraft Corp., 128 F.2d 632, 639-40, 53 U.S.P.Q. 563, 569 (2d Cir. 1942) (Frank, J., concurring); Marconi Wireless Co. v. United States, 320 U.S. 1, 60-61, 57 U.S.P.Q. 471, 496-98 (1943) (Frankfurter, J., dissenting). See also, Jungersen v. Ostby & Barton Co., 335 U.S. 560, 571-72, 80 U.S.P.Q. 32, 36 (1949) (Jackson, J., dissenting).

[31.4] General Tire & Rubber Co. v. Jefferson Chemical Co., 497 F.2d 1283, 182 U.S.P.Q. 70 (2d Cir. 1974) (Friendly, J.), *rev'g* 363 F. Supp. 871, 183 U.S.P.Q. 513 (S.D.N.Y. 1973), *cert. denied* 419 U.S. 968 (1974).

PAGE 122

[Add new text at end of the section:]

While determinations of the obviousness or unobviousness of a claimed invention are to be based upon "the subject matter as a whole," where unobviousness is predicated upon an unusual or surprising result or advantage, such result or advantage must at least be mentioned in the specification.[32.1] Accordingly, a prima facie obvious product could not be rendered nonobvious by resorting to product advantages not disclosed in the specification.[32.2] Similarly, it was held that the patentee could not support the patent by the fact that its actual device, as made and sold, was superior in ways neither related to nor shown on the record to follow from the patent claims.[32.3] Patentability may not be based on an undisclosed "inherent" feature that could be discovered only by building the assembly described in the patent specification and testing it.[32.4] At least one court has gone so far as to strongly suggest that the advantage or unexpected result upon which unobviousness is based must not only be adverted to in the specification but must also be mentioned in the claims.[32.5]

There is no need to determine the level of ordinary skill in the art where there are in fact no differences between the prior art and the claims at issue.[32.6]

A problem sometimes encountered is determining which is the relevant art. Thus, a U.S. district court held invalid claims to a patent addressed to the use of an epoxy resin to bond railroad rails, even though the patentability of these claims had been passed upon by the Patent Office Board of Appeals. The court took the position that the Board erred in gauging patentability by the level of skill in the railroading art rather than in the technology of organic resins. The court noted that the technological backwardness of the railroad industry was notorious.[32.7] In another case the use of epoxy resins to bond zinc components was held obvious.[32.8]

[32.1] Graham v. John Deere Co., 383 U.S. 1, 23, 148 U.S.P.Q. 459, 469 (1966); United States v. Adams, 383 U.S. 39, 48-49, 148 U.S.P.Q. 479, 482 (1966).

[32.2] General Tire & Rubber Co. v. Jefferson Chemical Co., 497 F.2d 1283, 1289, 182 U.S.P.Q. 70, 74 (2d Cir. 1974), *rev'g* 363 F. Supp. 871, 183 U.S.P.Q. 513 (S.D.N.Y. 1973), *cert. denied* 419 U.S. 968 (1974).

[32.3] Julie Laboratories, Inc. v. Guideline Instruments, Inc., 501 F.2d 1131, 1135, 183 U.S.P.Q. 1, 4 (2d Cir. 1974). See also, Iron Ore Co. v. Dow Chemical Co., 500 F.2d 189, 194, 182 U.S.P.Q. 520, 523 (10th Cir. 1974).

[32.4] Maclaren v. B-I-W Group, 535 F.2d 1367, 1374, 190 U.S.P.Q. 513, 518 (2d Cir. 1976).

[32.5] Koppers Co. v. S & S Corrugated Paper Machinery Co., 517 F.2d 1182, 1188, 185 U.S.P.Q. 705, 710 (2d Cir. 1975).

[32.6] Trico Products Corp. v. Robert Co., 490 F.2d 1280, 1281-82, 180 U.S.P.Q. 289, 290 (2d Cir. 1973), *cert. denied* 417 U.S. 933 (1974).

[32.7] Allegheny Drop Forge Co. v. Portec, Inc., 370 F. Supp. 673, 181 U.S.P.Q. 810 (W.D.Pa. 1974).

[32.8] Rex Chainbilt, Inc. v. Harco Products, Inc, 181 U.S.P.Q. 432 (C.D.Cal. 1973).

§ 3.   Rebuttal of Prima Facie Obviousness

PAGE 122

[*In seventh text line of first paragraph of this section, add after* "as its solution.":]

Whether all the objects of the invention enumerated in the specification have been satisfied by the prior art is germane to a conclusion of obviousness;[32.9] however, the fact that prior art is directed to the same problem as is the invention in question is not dispositive of obviousness.[32.10] In the law of patents it is the last step that counts.[32.11]

[32.9] Vollrath Co. v. Premium Plastics, Inc., 385 F. Supp. 843, 183 U.S.P.Q. 335, 338 (N.D.Ill. 1974).

[32.10] *In re* Donovan, 509 F.2d 554, 184 U.S.P.Q. 414 (C.C.P.A. 1975).

[32.11] The Barbed Wire Patent, 143 U.S. 275, 283 (1891).

[*Add text following paragraph numbered* "(2)":]

A prima facie case of obviousness is established where the teachings of the prior art appear to suggest the claimed subject matter to persons of ordinary skill in the art. Once a primer case has been made out by the Patent Office, it is incumbent upon the applicant to go forward with the objective evidence of unobviousness. When evidence to rebut a prima facie case of obviousness is submitted, the burden of going forward shifts to the Patent Office. Whether the applicant's burden of going forward to rebut a prima facie case of obviousness has been successfully carried out requires that the entire path to the decision be retraced. Prima facie obviousness is a conclusion of law, not of the facts. Facts established by rebuttal evidence must be evaluated with facts on which conclusion of prima facie obviousness was reached, and not against that earlier conclusion itself.[32.12]

Numerous situations which have been deemed to constitute a case of prima facie obviousness correspond to or parallel one of the older negative rules of invention. Thus a situation which amounted to the scaling up of a prior art process, that is, mere use of commercial quantities, was deemed prima facie obvious.[32.13] The substitution of a slot/detent for a hook/detent locking mechanism was deemed to be a mere design change or substitution of obvious equivalents that drew from mere mechanical skills.[32.14] It would be incongruous for one manufacturer to be able to exact license fees from other manufacturers by being the first to describe the *logical use* of machinery; producing an old product by closely analogous use of old machine and process is not patentable.[32.15]

[32.12] *In re* Rinehart, 531 F.2d 1048, 1052 189 U.S.P.Q. 143, 147 (C.C.P.A. 1976).
[32.13] *In re* Rinehart, N.32.12 *supra.*
[32.14] Kaspar Wire Works, Inc. v. Leco Engineering & Machine, Inc., 190 U.S.P.Q. 85, 88 (M.D.Fla. 1976).
[32.15] Grain Products, Inc. v. Lincoln Grain, Inc., 191 U.S.P.Q. 177, 180 (S.D.Ind. 1976).

[Penultimate paragraph on page 122 now reads:]

Just how much difference the difference must make to be unobvious is incapable of mechanical or general formulation. Each case must ultimately turn on its own peculiar facts. Whether obvious claims have been allowed to other applicants is immaterial.[32.16] Where the claimed structure is simple and/or differs only slightly from the prior art, the inquiry may focus upon the utility or result effected.

[32.16] *In re* Giolito, 530 F.2d 397, 400, 188 U.S.P.Q. 645, 648 (C.C.P.A. 1976).

[Add new text after last line on the page:]

The Supreme Court's most recent decision involving Section 103 involved a patent directed to a combination of old elements on a water flush system for removing cow manure from a sloped floor of a dairy barn. Apparently the closest applicable prior art involved spot delivery of water from tanks or pools to a sloped barn floor by means of high pressure hoses or pipes.[34.1]

The novelty of the Gribble and Bennett system resided in the *abrupt* release in a cascade or surge of water from tanks or pools *directly* onto the barn floor, without first passing through pipes or hoses. The results attained by the patentees Gribble and Bennett were unlike anything previously attained (excepting Hercules in cleaning the Augean stables, which was actually alluded to by the Court) in that they did not require any supplemental hand labor. The Supreme Court, nevertheless, held the patent invalid as failing to satisfy the unobviousness standard of Section 103. The rationale for the Court's holding was that all the claimed elements were old and that it is not unobvious simply to rearrange old elements so that each performs the same function it had been known to perform in the prior art, even though the rearrangement produces a more dramatic or striking result than previous combinations.

Slight reflection, however, should make it apparent that there has not been an invention yet made that does not amount to a combination of old elements. This is as true of chemical arts as of the mechanical arts, although perhaps in inventions involving the latter, that fact is less patent (and thus, perhaps, more likely patentable) in the Court's mind. Even a new chemical element is but a combination of old electrons, protons and neutrons. In its opinion, the Court suggests that whatever it characterizes as a combination of old elements can meet the unobviousness standard of Section 103 only where the combination produces a new or different function. No clue, however, is given as to what type of change might in the Court's opinion constitute a new or different function. The Supreme Court, moreover, disagreed with the Court of Appeals' finding that results attained by the Gribble and Bennett System could be characterized as synergistic. Perhaps of significance is the fact that after the Court of Appeals held the patent valid (reversing the District Court) the alleged infringer petitioned for a new trial on the ground of newly discovered evidence, but this the Court of Appeals refused to allow as not having been timely presented. It should also be noted that the novelty involved in the Gribble and Bennett System appears to reside in a method rather than in a system (or apparatus) as it was claimed.[34.2]

Not surprisingly, lower courts have experienced difficulties in grappling with the Supreme Court's guidelines on the patentability of claims drawn to a combination of old elements (sometimes referred to as "combination patents" or "combination inventions"). Thus, one district court stated that, on one hand, where the improvement is claimed to result from a combination of elements present in the prior art, patentable invention is somewhat elusive, while on the hand, there may still be combination patents that are valid in that the results they obtain are so superior to the prior art and so nonobvious from the mere assembly of old elements that the use of the whole operation first becomes practical. Apparently, one factor in determining whether a combination of separate prior art elements is deemed to be unobvious is whether those elements actually interact or cooperate rather than merely co-exist in aggregate.[34.3]

It is not enough to integrate old elements into a single structure; rather, it must be found that the new device was an unusual or surprising consequence of the unification of old elements.[34.4]

A mere aggregation or amalgam of old elements is not patentable.[34.5] Where it was found that a combination of old elements produced a result that those skilled in the field, based on prior knowledge of functions of individual elements, would not have expected, a patent drawn to such combination of old elements was held to be valid.[34.6]

The Supreme Court's avowed policy on patentability has been expressed in the following terms: "He who seeks to build a better mousetrap today has a long path to tread before reaching the Patent Office."[34.7] That comment on "mousetraps" notwithstanding, the Eighth Circuit Court of Appeals held claims to a patent on an animal trap valid and infringed. It marked the first time that a court held a patent valid since the enactment of the present Patent Act.[34.8]

It has been said that there is no legally recognizable or protected "essential" element, "gist," or "heart" of invention in a combination patent.[34.9] Nevertheless, it is submitted that the gist of a "combination patent" is the *combination itself,* that is, the manner in which the elements are brought into concert and the result that combination is capable of achieving relative to the results achieved by the isolated components.

In attempting to apply the Supreme Court's guidelines on unobviousness a threshold question in the minds of many courts is whether or not the alleged invention is a "combination invention."[34.10] As explained above, however, every invention is a "combination invention."

[34.1] Sakraida v. Ag Pro, Inc., 425 U.S. 273, 189 U.S.P.Q. 449, *rehearing denied* 426 U.S. 955 (1976).

[34.2] Sakraida v. Ag Pro., N.34.1 *supra.*

[34.3] Sargent Industries, Inc. v. Sundstrand Corp., 189 U.S.P.Q. 225, 231-32 (N.D.Ill. 1975).

[34.4] St. Regis Paper Co. v. Winchester Carton Corp., 410 F. Supp. 1304, 1307, 189 U.S.P.Q. 514, 516 (D.Mass. 1976).

[34.5] Aluminum Company of America v. Amerola Products Corp., 191 U.S.P.Q. 363 (W.D.Pa. 1976).

34.6 Clopay Corp. v. Blessings Corp., 422 F. Supp. 1312, 191 U.S.P.Q. 751 (D.Del. 1976).
34.7 Graham v. John Deere Co., 383 U.S. 1, 19, 148 U.S.P.Q. 459, 467 (1966).
34.8 Woodstream Corp. v. Herter's, Inc., 446 F.2d 1143, 170 U.S.P.Q. 380 (8th Cir. 1971), *rev'g* 312 F. Supp. 369, 165 U.S.P.Q. 609 (D.Minn. 1970).
34.9 High Voltage Engineering Corp. v. Potentials, Inc., 398 F. Supp. 18, 20, 188 U.S.P.Q. 535, 536 (W.D.Tex. 1974).
34.10 Forbro Design Corp. v. Raytheon Corp., 532 F.2d 758, 760, 190 U.S.P.Q. 49, 51 (1st Cir. 1976).

PAGE 123

[In fifth text line of first paragraph, add after sentence ending in footnote 36:]

The fact that the patent is *an improvement* over other patents will not necessarily save it.[36.1] It matters not that the device works *better than* the prior art device if the improvement would have been obvious to those skilled in the art.[36.2]

36.1 Spound v. Mohasco Industries, Inc., 534 F.2d 404, 409, 190 U.S.P.Q. 1, 5 (1st Cir. 1976).
36.2 Airlite Plastics Co. v. Plastilite Corp., 526 F.2d 1078, 1082, 189 U.S.P.Q. 327, 330 (8th Cir. 1975).

[Insert text between first and second paragraphs:]

That the prior art teaches away from what is claimed militates against a finding of obviousness.[41.1] Doing what the prior art references try to avoid is the very antithesis of obviousness.[41.2] However, a prior art warning to "be careful" was not deemed equivalent to uniform prior art teaching that any investigation would be purposeless.[41.3]

41.1 Tights, Inc. v. Acme-McCrary Corp., 541 F.2d 1047, 1059, 191 U.S.P.Q. 305, 313 (4th Cir. 1976); Milgo Electronics Corp. v. United Telecommunications, Inc., 189 U.S.P.Q. 160, 168 (D.Kan. 1976).
41.2 *In re* Buehler, 515 F.2d 1134, 1141, 185 U.S.P.Q. 781, 787 (C.C.P.A. 1975).
41.3 Airtex Corp. v. Shelley Radiant Ceiling Co., 536 F.2d 145, 153, 190 U.S.P.Q. 6, 13 (7th Cir. 1976).

§ 3[3]. Synergism

PAGE 127

[Add new text at end of the section:]

It was held that a "synergistic" effect between materials in a new combination, sufficient to cross the legal border from a combination that merely produces a more striking result to one that constituted patentable invention, was demonstrated where the patented wire's insulation temperature rating was unpredictably high as compared to the temperature ratings of its components and was unexpectedly flame resistant.[52.1]

[52.1] International Telephone & Telegraph Corp. v. Raychem Corp., 538 F.2d 453, 457-58, 191 U.S.P.Q. 1, 4-5 (1st Cir. 1976).

[Add new Sections: §§ 3[4] and 3[5].]

[4] Chemical Process

The novelty of a starting material may lend unobviousness to a method of use. The use of a new microorganism in an old and presumably obvious process was held unobvious.[52.2] It is improper to determine obviousness of a three-step process by merely asking whether given the product of two unobvious claimed steps, the third claimed step of using that product would have been obvious. Obviousness of invention as a whole, which includes two unobvious first steps, must be determined.[52.3]

[5] Physical Mixtures

In regard to physical mixtures of ingredients, unobviousness may reside not only in the ingredients themselves but also in the particular manner in which they are to be combined or associated. A physical mixture of ingredients useful in treating some of the symptoms of overindulgence in alcohol was held patentable, notwithstanding that each ingredient was known to be effective for the specific purpose intended, because the claim called for the physical division or segregation of the mixture into two defined separate portions. This division enhanced the stability and the shelf-life of the overall composition. The manner in which the ingredients were separated was novel and deemed unobvious. Although the patent specification disclosed separate *encapsulation* of the two portions, claims calling merely for the division into two separate portions were deemed to define the invention.[52.4]

[52.2] *In re* Mancy, 499 F.2d 1289, 1293, 182 U.S.P.Q. 303, 306 (C.C.P.A. 1974); *In re* Kuehl, 475 F.2d 658, 664, 177 U.S.P.Q. 250, 255 (C.C.P.A. 1973).

52.3 *In re* Hirao, 535 F.2d 67, 68-69, 190 U.S.P.Q. 15, 17 (C.C.P.A. 1976).
52.4 *In re* Rice, 481 F.2d 1316, 178 U.S.P.Q. 478 (C.C.P.A. 1973).

§ 4. The Subtests of Invention

PAGE 128

[Add to text immediately after quotation from the Supreme Court:]

Lower courts in upholding patent validity not infrequently buttress that conclusion with a finding of commercial success, long-felt but unresolved need, the failure of others, and/or commercial acquiescence. These secondary considerations are signposts of patentability and are properly deemed infinitely more reliable than a prior evaluation aided by hindsight.[56.1]

A court of appeals reversed a district court's holding of patent invalidity at least in part because the evidence showed that others skilled in the field had been unable to find a satisfactory solution. This, the appellate court stated, is a "weighty indication that at the *then* level of skill . . . the patented discovery was not obvious."[56.2]

[56.1] Lerner v. Child Guidance Products, Inc., 406 F. Supp. 560, 565-66, 189 U.S.P.Q. 83, 88 (S.D.N.Y. 1975).

An affirmative finding of at least one of the "supports of patentability" was made in each of the following cases in which patent validity was upheld: International Telephone & Telegraph Corp. v. Raychem Corp., 538 F.2d 453, 191 U.S.P.Q. 1 (1st Cir. 1976), *aff'g* 188 U.S.P.Q. 214 (D.Mass. 1975); Tights, Inc. v. Acme-McCrary Corp., 541 F.2d 1047, 191 U.S.P.Q. 305 (4th Cir. 1976); Eutectic Corp. v. Metco, Inc., 418 F. Supp. 1186, 191 U.S.P.Q. 505 (E.D.N.Y. 1976); St. Regis Paper Co. v. Bemis Co., 403 F. Supp. 776, 188 U.S.P.Q. 107 (S.D.Ill. 1975).

[56.2] Coal-Fin Electronics Corp. v. International Corp., 491 F.2d 660, 663, 180 U.S.P.Q. 481, 483 (9th Cir. 1974).

In the following cases, the patent was held invalid notwithstanding the submission of evidence of the presence of at least one of the "signposts of patentability": Airtex Corp. v. Shelley Radiant Ceiling Co., 536 F.2d 145, 190 U.S.P.Q. 6 (7th Cir. 1976); Norwood v. Ehrenreich Photo-Optical Industries, Inc., 529 F.2d 3, 189 U.S.P.Q. 196 (9th Cir. 1975); Koppers Co. v. S. & S. Corrugated Paper Machine Co., 510 F.2d 360, 185 U.S.P.Q. 705 (2d Cir.), *cert. denied* 421 U.S. 998 (1974); Vanity Fair Mills, Inc. v. Olga Co., 510 F.2d 336, 184 U.S.P.Q. 643 (2d Cir. 1975).

§ 4[1]. Commercial Success

PAGE 129

[Add at end of the section:]

The fact that only one licensee exists has been taken as evidence *against* commercial success.[57.1]

[57.1] CMI Corp. v. Lakeland Construction Co., 184 U.S.P.Q. 721, 726 (N.D.Ill. 1975).

§ 4[2].   Long-felt Demand

PAGE 129

[Add text after last paragraph in the section:]

Long-felt demand tends to establish unobviousness, while prompt invention once the need becomes apparent tends to establish obviousness.[58.1] Similarly, generally contemporaneous and independent completion of the invention by another is taken, by some courts, as evidence that the invention was not beyond the reach of those of ordinary skill in the art.[58.2]

[58.1] Continental Oil Co. v. Witco Chemical Corp., 484 F.2d 777, 782, 179 U.S.P.Q. 200, 203 (7th Cir. 1973); Potter Instrument Co. v. Bucode, Inc., 184 U.S.P.Q. 662, 670 (E.D.N.Y. 1975); H.K. Porter Co. v. Black & Decker Mfg. Co., 182 U.S.P.Q. 401, 414 (N.D.Ill. 1974).

[58.2] Kaz Manufacturing Co. v. Northern Electric Co., 412 F. Supp. 470, 483, 189 U.S.P.Q. 464, 476 (S.D.N.Y. 1976); Stadium, Inc. v. Polycraft Corp., 191 U.S.P.Q. 710, 715 (N.D.Ill. 1976); Lerner v. Child Guidance Products, Inc., 406 F. Supp 560, 566, 189 U.S.P.Q. 83, 89 (S.D.N.Y. 1975); Westwood Chemical, Inc. v. Dow Corning Corp., 189 U.S.P.Q. 649, 678 (E.D.Mich. 1975); Potter Instrument Co. v. ODEC Computer Systems, Inc., 370 F. Supp. 198, 204, 181 U.S.P.Q. 572, 575-76 (D.R.I. 1974).

§ 4[3].   Commercial Acquiescence

PAGE 130

[Add after last line of text on the page:]

Also said to constitute persuasive circumstantial evidence of nonobviousness, at least in respect to designs, is copying itself.[60.1]

[60.1] H.K. Porter Co. v. Black & Decker Mfg. Co., Inc., 182 U.S.P.Q. 401, 414 (N.D.Ill. 1974).

Notes

PAGE 131

[Add to footnote 7:]

In re Nomiya, 509 F.2d 566, 571, 184 U.S.P.Q. 607, 612-13 (C.C.P.A. 1975); Clopay Corp. v. Blessings Corp., 422 F. Supp. 1312, 1317, 191 U.S.P.Q. 751, 759 (D.Del. 1976), citing PATENT LAW FUNDAMENTALS as authority.

[Add to footnote 28:]

Deering Milliken Research Corp. v. Beaunit Corp., 538 F.2d 1022, 1025, 189 U.S.P.Q. 565, 567 (4th Cir.), *cert. denied* 426 U.S. 936 (1976); Airlite Plastics Co. v. Plastilite Corp., 526 F.2d 1078, 1080, 189 U.S.P.Q. 327, 328 (8th Cir. 1975); Parker v. Motorola, Inc., 524 F.2d 518, 531, 188 U.S.P.Q. 225, 235 (5th Cir.), *cert. denied* 427 U.S. 908 (1976); Deyerle v. Wright Mfg. Co., 496 F.2d 45, 52, 181 U.S.P.Q. 685, 690 (6th Cir. 1974).

[Add to footnote 34:]

Sakraida v. Ag Pro, Inc., 425 U.S. 273, 282, 189 U.S.P.Q. 449, 453, *rehearing denied* 426 U.S. 955 (1976); Parker v. Motorola, Inc., 524 F.2d 518, 531-32, 188 U.S.P.Q. 225, 236 (5th Cir. 1975), *cert. denied* 427 U.S. 908 (1976); Kaspar Wire Works, Inc. v. Leco Engineering and Machine, Inc., 190 U.S.P.Q. 85, 91 (M.D.Fla. 1976).

PAGE 132

[Add to footnote 38:]

In re Clinton, 188 U.S.P.Q. 365, 367 (C.C.P.A. 1976).

[Add to footnote 44:]

In re Waymouth, 499 F.2d 1273, 182 U.S.P.Q. 290 (C.C.P.A. 1974).

[Add to footnote 46:]

In re Mercier, 515 F.2d 1161, 1167, 185 U.S.P.Q. 774, 779 (C.C.P.A. 1975).

[Add to footnote 49:]

The following cases in effect take the position structurally obvious compounds may be patentable where one or more unobvious properties have been discovered: Pfizer, Inc. v. International Rectifier Corp., 538 F.2d 180, 188-89, 190 U.S.P.Q. 273, 280-81 (8th Cir. 1976); *In re* Regel, 526 F.2d 1399, 188 U.S.P.Q. 136 (C.C.P.A. 1975); *In re* Stemniski, 444 F.2d 581, 179 U.S.P.Q. 343 (C.C.P.A. 1974); *In re* Wiggins, 488 F.2d 538, 179 U.S.P.Q. 421 (C.C.P.A. 1973); Commissioner v. Deutsche Gold-und-Silber Scheideanstalt, 397 F.2d 656, 157 U.S.P.Q. 549 (D.D.C. 1968).

The following cases take the position that discovery of a property or properties of a structurally obvious compound does not render such compound patentable: Brown v. Gottschalk, 484 F.2d 813, 179 U.S.P.Q. 65 (D.C.C. 1973); Monsanto v. Rohm & Haas Co., 312 F. Supp. 778, 164 U.S.P.Q. 556 (E.D.Pa. 1970), *aff'd* 456 F.2d 592, 172 U.S.P.Q. 323 (3d Cir. 1972), *cert. denied* 409 U.S. 899 (1972).

Chapter 9

PRIORITY OF INVENTION

§ 1. Determination of Priority

§ 1[1]. Conception

PAGE 136

[Add to text at end of the section:]

Conception involves not merely the perception or realization of the desirability of producing a certain result. Rather, it involves the perception or realization of *means by which* the result can be produced. Conception, which is the mental possession of means by which a desired result can be effected, must be such that the completion or effectuation of the invention requires *no more than routine skill.* Extensive subsequent research will negate earlier asserted date of conception.[1.1] Conception is established by showing formation in the inventor's mind of a definite and permanent idea of the complete and operative invention as it is thereafter to be applied in practice. Utility is a necessary ingredient of conception.[1.2] Conception of a process does not begin with observation of phenomenon, but rather necessarily includes contemporaneous recognition of the application of the observed phenomenon and a disclosure to others sufficient to enable practice of the invention.[1.3]

The conception of the idea of a complete and operative invention must be proven by evidence that the inventors were in possession of such idea and that the corroborating witness understood what was the invention of the counts.[1.4] There can be no conception or reduction to practice of new form, or process of using new form, of otherwise old composition of matter, for the purpose of establishing priority in interference, without recognition or appreciation of new form's existence.[1.5]

[1.1] Bell Telephone Laboratories, Inc. v. Hughes Aircraft Co., 191 U.S.P.Q. 23, 29 (D.Del. 1976).

[1.2] Rebstock v. Flouret, 191 U.S.P.Q. 342, 344 (Bd.Pat.Int. 1975).

[1.3] Anderson v. Anderson, 403 F. Supp. 834, 845, 188 U.S.P.Q. 194, 202-203 (D.D.C. 1975).

[1.4] Emery v. Ronden, 188 U.S.P.Q. 264, 267 (Bd.Pat.Int. 1974).

[1.5] Meitzner v. Corte, 537 F.2d 524, 528, 190 U.S.P.Q. 407, 410 (C.C.P.A. 1976).

PAGE 137

[In third text line, add after sentence ending in footnote 2:]

In the case of a product producing process, reduction to practice requires the establishment of a utility for products produced by the process.[2.1]

[2.1] Bell Telephone Laboratories, Inc. v. Hughes Aircraft Co., 191 U.S.P.Q. 23, 30 (D.Del. 1976); Azar v. Burns, 188 U.S.P.Q. 601, 604 (Bd.Pat.Int. 1975).

[In sixth text line, add after sentence ending in footnote 3:]

A composition of matter cannot be actually reduced to practice unless it has practical utility.[3.1] To establish a prima facie case of actual reduction to practice of a compound, applicant must establish that he knew of a practical utility of his compound.[3.2]

[3.1] Azar v. Burns, 188 U.S.P.Q. 601, 604 (Bd.Pat.Int. 1975).
[3.2] Golborn v. Weil, 189 U.S.P.Q. 95, 99 (Bd.Pat.Int. 1975).

[Add after first full text paragraph on page 137:]

The same standards of proof of utility are applicable to a constructive reduction to practice as are applicable to an actual reduction to practice.[5.1]

[5.1] Blicharz v. Hays, 496 F.2d 603, 181 U.S.P.Q. 712 (C.C.P.A. 1974); Anderson v. Natta, 480 F.2d 1392, 178 U.S.P.Q. 458 (C.C.P.A. 1973); Triaaiani v. Halva, 178 U.S.P.Q. 372 (Bd.Pat.Int. 1973).

[In sixth line of third full text paragraph, add after "evidence of conception.":*]*

Two definitions of active reduction to practice exist: under one, reduction to practice is not reached until a physical embodiment of the invention or model has been tested sufficiently to demonstrate its utility, including tests to put the invention into definitive form and to see whether the conception is worth exploiting; and under the other definition of actual reduction to practice, the mere existence of the physical model is equated with reduction to practice with tests for utility following.[7.1]

[7.1] *In re* Yarn Processing Patent Validity Litigation, 401 F. Supp. 673, 675-76, 189 U.S.P.Q. 598, 600-601 (S.D.Fla. 1976).

[Add text immediately preceding last paragraph on the page (paragraph running over to page 138):]

Thus, it was held that a disposable diaper need not have been tested on an infant where tests actually employed were "reasonably certain."[8.1] A fail-safe parachute was not required to have been tested under actual flight conditions.[8.2] In regard to compositions of matter, it has been held that a reduction to practice was established merely by demonstrating a similarity of properties of the new composition to establish properties of a known class of compositions having known utility, without the need to be tested at all.[8.3] Moreover, when an interference count does not recite any particular utility, evidence establishing a substantial utility for any purpose is sufficient to prove reduction to practice.[8.4]

To constitute an actual reduction to practice, the invention need not be perfect or incapable of further improvement.[8.5] An invention to be actually reduced to practice need not pass the testing with flying colors.[8.6] It is not necessary for actual reduction to practice that the invention was constructed and tested to be capable of commercial exploitation without further refinement.[8.7] A single successful use of the invention is sufficient to establish its actual reduction to practice.[8.8] However, an actual reduction to practice requires a showing of invention's embodiment in tangible form that shows every element of the invention defined in the count.[8.9] The inventors need not personally construct and test the invention.[8.10]

[8.1] Gellert v. Wanberg, 495 F.2d 779, 181 U.S.P.Q. 648 (C.C.P.A. 1974).
[8.2] Stencel v. Nordine, 481 F.2d 916, 178 U.S.P.Q. 625 (C.C.P.A. 1973).
[8.3] Silvestri v. Grant, 496 F.2d 593, 181 U.S.P.Q. 706, *cert. denied* 420 U.S. 928 (1975).
[8.4] Ciric v. Flanigen, 511 F.2d 1182, 1185, 185 U.S.P.Q. 103, 105 (C.C.P.A. 1975).
[8.5] Cochran v. Kresock, 530 F.2d 385, 391, 188 U.S.P.Q. 553 (C.C.P.A. 1976).
[8.6] *In re* Dardick, 496 F.2d 1234, 1238, 181 U.S.P.Q. 834, 837 (C.C.P.A. 1974).
[8.7] Mattor v. Coolegem, 530 F.2d 1391, 1395, 189 U.S.P.Q. 201, 204 (C.C.P.A. 1976).
[8.8] Beck v. Teague, 534 F.2d 300, 305, 189 U.S.P.Q. 625, 629 (C.C.P.A. 1976).
[8.9] Meitzner v. Corte, 537 F.2d 524, 530, 190 U.S.P.Q. 407, 412 (C.C.P.A. 1976).
[8.10] Eutectic Corp. v. Metco, Inc., 191 U.S.P.Q. 505, 518 (E.D.N.Y. 1976); Tucker v. Becker, 188 U.S.P.Q. 260, 263 (Bd.Pat.Int. 1975).

§ 1[3]. Diligence

PAGE 139

[Add text immediately preceding first full paragraph on the page:]

A party charged with showing diligence must account for the entire period during which diligence is required. Reasonable diligence may be shown by affirmative acts toward reduction to practice or reasons for failing to act. Reasonable diligence by the inventor must be corroborated. Merely asserting diligence does not factually establish it. A showing of diligence must include a showing of what acts occurred as well as the specific dates on which they occurred. An affidavit, filed to corroborate diligence, which states conclusions of law as opposed to facts, is entitled to little weight.[23.1] The testimony of the inventor(s) alone is usually deemed insufficient in establishing diligence. While day-to-day corroboration of an inventor's testimony regarding his activity during the period of diligence would be desirable, its absence is not fatal. Where lack of activity was attributed to "budgetary limits" and the "availability of animals" to test the conception, there was an affirmative duty to show just what they were in order to determine whether the delay was reasonable in light of these factors.[23.3]

[23.1] Rebstock v. Flouret, 191 U.S.P.Q. 342, 344 (Bd.Pat.Int. 1975).

[23.2] Bell Telephone Laboratories, Inc. v. Hughes Aircraft Co., 191 U.S.P.Q. 23, 31 (D.Del. 1976).

[23.3] Litchfield v. Eigen, 535 F.2d 72, 76-77, 190 U.S.P.Q. 113, 116 (C.C.P.A. 1976).

PAGE 140

[*Insert between second and third text paragraphs:*]

Commercialization is not a requirement for diligence, conception, or reduction to practice.[30.1]

[30.1] Vancil v. Arata, 191 U.S.P.Q. 464, 466 (Bd.Pat.Int. 1976).

PAGE 141

[*Add text at end of §1[3] after* "C prevails against A!":]

IV. A party that was the first to reduce to practice, but thereafter suppressed or concealed his invention, forfeited the right to rely on his date of actual reduction to practice. Such right cannot be resurrected by thereafter taking steps to file a patent application, even though such steps were taken before an opponent's entry into the field. Where there is a delay between actual reduction to practice and filing of a patent application and delay is determined to be "unreasonable," there is a basis for inferring an intent to suppress or conceal.[31.1] Knowledge of an opponent's entry into the field is a factor to be considered in connection with the question of abandonment, concealment or suppression under Section 102(g).[31.2] The conduct of a corporate owner of the invention that exercised, with applicant's apparent approval, control over the invention, including decisions relating to the patent application, is relevant in determining whether the invention was suppressed or concealed.[31.3]

Where the basis of an award of priority is a foreign filing date, the losing party may nevertheless be entitled to a patent on obvious variations of the counts lost in the interference, provided the losing party's U.S. filing date is earlier than the prevailing party's actual U.S. filing date.[31.4]

A   X
                    U.S. filing
                      date

B   X _____ X
           5/1/63   10/6/63
        Foreign Filing   U.S. Filing
           date   date

B will prevail in an interference with A but B's disclosure is not effective as prior art until B's actual U.S. filing date.

[31.1] Adler v. Hair, 188 U.S.P.Q. 186, 189 (Bd.Pat.Int. 1975).
[31.2] Lewis v. Birle, 189 U.S.P.Q. 91, 92 (Bd.Pat.Int. 1975).
[31.3] Adler v. Hair, 188 U.S.P.Q. 186, 188 (Bd.Pat.Int. 1975).
[31.4] In re McKellin, 529 F.2d 1324, 188 U.S.P.Q. 428 (C.C.P.A. 1975).

§ 2. Adjudication

PAGE 142

[In fourth line of second full text paragraph, add after sentence ending in footnote 34:]

Joint inventors cannot corroborate each other's testimony as to conception and reduction to practice.[34.1]

[34.1] Anderson v. Anderson, 403 F. Supp. 834, 846, 188 U.S.P.Q. 194, 203 (D.D.C. 1975).

[In eighth line of second full paragraph, add after "established.":*]*

The burden of proof of an inventor's alleged conception and reduction to practice is a heavy one requiring full corroboration by other than the inventor's own self-serving testimony or records.[34.2]

[34.2] Lockheed Aircraft Corp. v. United States, 190 U.S.P.Q. 134, 139 (Ct.Cl. 1976).

PAGE 143

[Insert immediately preceding first full text paragraph:]

In regard to the need for corroboration, the Court of Customs & Patent Appeals has adopted what it has denominated a "rule of reason approach": every element of a count must be corroborated but there is no single, fixed corroboration formula. Documents and other activities may be corroborative. The testimony of one who witnessed and understood a compound's actual reduction to practice is strong evidence, but its absence need not be fatal when other evidence is sufficient to corroborate actual reduction to practice.[35.1]

Thus, it has been said that a corroborating witness need not, in every case, have independent recollection of each and every individual experiment that he may have seen, particularly where eyewitness testimony is not relied upon as sole corroborating evidence that the experiment was conducted. Dated signature on notebook page of witness sufficiently familiar with the particular field of technology to understand what is described on that page is evidence, under *rule* of *reason,* upon which one may find corroboration.[35.2] Corroboration is not a ritual but a method for determining the veracity of testimony. An inventor's testimony is evidence, its weight a function of his credibility. One method of establishing credibility is by a corroborating witness, but it is not the only method.[35.3] It was held, however, that the mere statement by witnesses that they "witnessed the completion and progress of the experimental work described" in certain exhibits was deemed insufficient to corroborate the structure of any compound prepared by applicant.[35.4]

That twenty-five embodiments of the invention had been ordered, without any evidence that the order had been filled, was deemed insufficient to establish an actual reduction to practice. Also, such a small quantity was taken as a possible indication that the purchase might well have been for test purposes.[35.5]

50 PATENT LAW FUNDAMENTALS

35.1 Miller v. Wachtel, — F.2d —, —, 191 U.S.P.Q. 571, 574-75 (C.C.P.A. 1976).

35.2 Grasselli v. Dewing, 534 F.2d 306, 311, 189 U.S.P.Q. 637, 640-41 (C.C.P.A. 1976);
Mattor v. Coolegem, 530 F.2d 1391, 1394-95, 189 U.S.P.Q. 201, 203 (C.C.P.A. 1976);
Anderson v. Pieper, 442 F.2d 982, 985, 169 U.S.P.Q. 788, 790 (C.C.P.A. 1971).

35.3 Mattor v. Coolegem, 530 F.2d 1391, 1394-95, 189 U.S.P.Q. 201, 203 (C.C.P.A. 1976).

35.4 Golborn v. Weil, 189 U.S.P.Q. 95, 98 (Bd.Pat.Int. 1975).

35.5 Elliott v. Barker, 481 F.2d 1337, 1340, 179 U.S.P.Q. 100, 102 (C.C.P.A. 1973).

PAGE 144

[In fourth text line on the page, delete the period after sentence ending in footnote 38 and add the following:]

, except in an interference involving a patent, in which case the junior party has a burden of establishing his date of invention quite as absolute as in a criminal case, that is, "beyond a reasonable doubt."[38.1] The burden of proving derivation by a preponderance of evidence is on the party alleging it, whether he be a senior or junior party.[38.2] A junior party is not entitled to "judgment on the record" on the question of alleged derivation against a senior party who has not had an opportunity to rebut an alleged prima facie case of derivation.[38.3]

38.1 Harris v. NRM Corp., 191 U.S.P.Q. 643, 651 (N.D.Ohio 1976).

38.2 Anderson v. Anderson, 403 F. Supp. 834, 847, 188 U.S.P.Q. 194, 204 (D.D.C. 1975).

38.3 Inone v. Lobur, 189 U.S.P.Q. 61 (Bd.Pat.Int. 1975).

[Add immediately before first full text paragraph on the page:]

However, introduction into the United States of a true copy of the original invention disclosure that was prepared by an interference party, though in a foreign language, is tantamount to a conception of counts' invention in the United States by such interference party as of its date of introduction.[40.1] Receipt of knowledge of a foreign invention in the United States is tantamount to conception in the United States as of the date of receipt in the United States.[40.2]

40.1 Clevenger v. Kooi, 190 U.S.P.Q. 188 (Bd.Pat.Int. 1974).

40.2 Monaco v. Hoffman, 189 F. Supp. 474, 127 U.S.P.Q. 516 (D.D.C. 1960), *aff'd* 293 F.2d 883, 130 U.S.P.Q. 97 (D.C.C. 1961); Thomas v. Reese, 1880 C.D. 12 (Comm.Pat. 1880). In regard to Rule 131 affidavit, see Ex parte Pavilanus, 166 U.S.P.Q. 413 (P.O.Bd.App. 1969).

PAGE 146

[In eighth text line of first full paragraph, add after "copied claim.":]

A party raising or provoking an interference by copying claims has the burden of proof on the issue of enablement.[48.1]

[48.1] Snitzer v. Etzel, 531 F.2d 1062, 1066, 189 U.S.P.Q. 415, 417 (C.C.P.A. 1976).

PAGE 147

[In sixth text line of second full paragraph, add after sentence ending in footnote 53:]

Absent contrary evidence, a count must be given its broadest reasonable interpretation and should not be given a contrived, artificial, or narrow interpretation that fails to apply language of the count in its most obvious sense.[53.1] A count's terms should be given the broadest construction its language will reasonably bear, without reference to specification from which they originate.[53.2]

[53.1] Grasselli v. Dewing, 534 F.2d 306, 309, 189 U.S.P.Q. 637, 639 (C.C.P.A. 1976).
[53.2] Gold v. Armstrong, 189 U.S.P.Q. 93, 94 (Bd.Pat.Int. 1975).

PAGE 151

[Add text after last line on the page:]

The Board of Patent Interference must decide an issue of priority and issues ancillary to priority before it. It may not circumvent its responsibility by awarding priority "against" each party to the interference.[63.1] Where the Board is of the opinion that none of the parties before it is entitled to an award of priority, its proper course is to make a recommendation pursuant to Rule 259 (37 C.F.R. 1.259) to that effect.

The Board of Patent Interference also has authority to determine whether an interference in fact exists, although the issue may not be ancillary to priority. An interference in a fact situation exists where the patentee's claims and allowable claims of pending application are patentably indistinct.[63.2] An invention is not the language of a count but the subject matter thereby defined.[63.3] According to the Court of Customs & Patent Appeals, the question of whether an interference in fact exists may be an issue ancillary to priority.[63.4]

[63.1] Sheffner v. Gallo, 515 F.2d 1169, 185 U.S.P.Q. 726 (C.C.P.A. 1975).

63.2 Dewilde v. Leigh, 191 U.S.P.Q. 256 (Bd.Pat.Int. 1976).
63.3 Meitzner v. Corte, 537 F.2d 524, 530, 190 U.S.P.Q. 407, 412 (C.C.P.A. 1976).
63.4 Nitz v. Ehrenreich, 537 F.2d 539, 543, 190 U.S.P.Q. 413, 416-17 (C.C.P.A. 1976).

PAGE 152

[*In second text paragraph, add after sentence ending in footnote* **66:**]

Fraud is ancillary to the issue of priority of invention.[66.1] However, where review is before a federal district court under 35 U.S.C. 146, an issue of fraud not touching the question of priority of invention may not be raised for the first time.[66.2]

66.1 Spaiti v. Marsh, 191 U.S.P.Q. 684 (S.D.N.Y. 1976).
66.2 Standard Oil Co. v. Montedison, — F.2d —, 191 U.S.P.Q. 657 (3d Cir. 1976).

[*Insert between third and fourth text paragraphs:*]

Judgment is rendered by the Board of Patent Interferences, while termination by dissolution is within the jurisdiction of the primary examiner. The Board of Patent Interferences lacks the authority to dissolve an interference.[67.1]

67.1 Nitz v. Ehrenreich, 537 F.2d 539, 190 U.S.P.Q. 413, 417 (C.C.P.A. 1976).

[*In fourth text paragraph, add after sentence ending in footnote* **68:**]

Where parties to an interference failed to file a supplemental undertaking relating to the settlement of the interference, the patent was held invalid, even though the parties had filed the original interference settlement agreement.[68.1]

68.1 Moog, Inc. v. Pegasus Laboratories, Inc., 376 F. Supp. 439, 183 U.S.P.Q. 225 (E.D. Mich. 1974).

[*Add at end of fifth text paragraph:*]

If one party seeks review in the District Court, his choice of forum will prevail.

Notes

PAGE 154

[*Add to footnote* **5**:]

Ex parte Frank, 191 U.S.P.Q. 412, 413 (P.O.Bd.App. 1975).

[*Add to footnote* **28:**]

Bell Telephone Laboratories, Inc. v. Hughes Aircraft Co., 191 U.S.P.Q. 23, 25 (D.Del. 1976).

Chapter 10

THE INVENTORSHIP ENTITY
AND
EMPLOYER-EMPLOYEE RIGHTS

§ 1.   The Inventorship Entity

PAGE 158

[*In fifth text line of first paragraph in this section, add after* "inventors. The statutory basis . . . ":]

While inclusion of more or fewer than the true number of inventors in a patent renders it void, there is a presumption that the listing of inventors in an issued patent is correct. It is well established that since misjoinder is a technical defense, it must be proven by "clear and convincing" evidence.[1.1] That burden was satisfied in a case wherein the accused infringer successfully defended on the ground that he, and not the patentee, was the true inventor, even though the testimony of the accused infringer was uncorroborated by direct testimonial evidence.[1.2] Where it was established that the named inventor defrauded the Patent Office by claiming to be the sole inventor, the accused infringer was held entitled to an award of attorney's fees under Section 285.[1.3]

[1.1] Jamesbury Corp. v. United States, — F.2d —, 183 U.S.P.Q. 484, 488 (Ct.Cl. 1974).
[1.2] Campbell v. Spectrum Automation Co., 513 F.2d 932, 185 U.S.P.Q. 718 (6th Cir. 1975).
[1.3] Kramer v. Duralite Co., 181 U.S.P.Q. 326 (S.D.N.Y. 1973), *aff'd* 513 F.2d 932, 185 U.S.P.Q. 64 (2d Cir. 1975).

PAGE 159

[*Insert text after paragraph ending in footnote* 7:]

One who merely participated in the synthesis and testing of compositions under the oral instructions of the person who conceived them was deemed a joint inventor of such compositions.[7.1] The fact that one inventor made decisions as to what the invention should accomplish does not establish that it was his sole invention.[7.2]

[7.1] Mattor v. Coolegem, 530 F.2d 1391, 189 U.S.P.Q. 201, 204 (C.C.P.A. 1976).
[7.2] Tucker v. Naito, 188 U.S.P.Q. 260, 263 (Bd.Pat.Int. 1975).

§ 2. Nonjoinder and Misjoinder

PAGE 160

[*Add at end of first text paragraph in the section:*]

Where any misjoinder or nonjoinder is established, the tainted patent is invalid, even though only one of several inventors was erroneously added or omitted.[11.1]

[11.1] Grain Products, Inc. v. Lincoln Grain, Inc., 191 U.S.P.Q. 177 (S.D.Ind. 1976).

§ 3. Rights of Employer and Employee Inter Se

PAGE 163

[*Add immediately preceding first full text paragraph:*]

However, where a person expressly or impliedly contracts to devote his mental faculties and exercise his inventive ability for the benefit of his employer, the inventions conceived by him in the course of his employment and as a consequence of its pursuit belong in equity to the employer.[18.1]

[18.1] Prince Mfg., Inc. v. Automatic Partner, Inc., 191 U.S.P.Q. 450, 461 (N.J.Super.Ct., Ch.Div., MercerCty. 1976).

§ 4. An Employee's Obligations in Regard to His Employer's Trade Secrets

PAGE 164

[*Add immediately preceding last text paragraph on the page:*]

It has been held that the definition of a trade secret set out in *B.F. Goodrich Co. v. Wahlgemuth*[23.1] does not include a marketing concept or new product idea. The marketing concept involved was the use on notebook covers and binders of fashion designs and fabrics which matched clothing being advertised in young women's fashion magazines. Trade secret law is designed to protect a continuing competitive advantage, which a company enjoys due to confidential information it possesses, from destruction due to disclosure by a departed former employee. A marketing concept does not by confidentiality create a continuing competitive advantage because once it is implemented it is exposed for the world to see and for competitors to legally imitate.[23.2]

[23.1] 117 Ohio App. 493, 498-99, 137 U.S.P.Q. 804, 807 (1963).
[23.2] Richter v. Westab, Inc., 529 F.2d 896, 900, 189 U.S.P.Q. 321, 324 (6th Cir. 1976).

Chapter 11

GOVERNMENT INTEREST IN PATENTS: PROCUREMENT AND OWNERSHIP

§ 1. Inventions Made with Federal Funds

§ 1[1]. By Federal Employees

PAGE 169

[*Insert text immediately preceding last paragraph on the page (paragraph running over to page 170):*]

A United States district court held Executive Order 10096 unconstitutional, on the theory that the President, absent legislation indicating Congressional intent, lacked authority to alter the case law relating to the ownership of patent rights between employer and employee. The case law as announced in the *Dubilier* decision did not necessitate an assignment to the employer where employment called for no more than general research efforts.[1.1] The decision of the district court was reversed by the Seventh Circuit Court of Appeals, which held that Executive Order 10096 is constitutional.[1.2]

The rules governing the acquisition and protection of foreign rights by the United States including those inventions made by government employees, are set out in 37 C.F.R. 101.1-101.11.

[1.1] Kaplan v. Johnson, 189 U.S.P.Q. 501 (N.D.Ill. 1976).
[1.2] Kaplan v. Corcoran, — F.2d —, 192 U.S.P.Q. 129 (7th Cir. 1976).

§ 1[2]. By Nonfederal Employees

PAGE 172

[*Insert text immediately preceding last text paragraph of this section:*]

Problems arise not only in regard to the extent of the rights that belong to the government (patent or principal rights versus a license), but also in regard to the subject matter in which the government has an interest by virtue of the contract. Typically, contracts between the government and a private contractor will contain a "Patent Rights" clause, which will limit the acquisition of rights by the government under the contract to "subject inventions." A "subject invention" is generally defined as any invention conceived or first actually reduced to practice in the performance of the contract. Armed Services Procurement Regulations (ASPR), Section 9 (1949). The Court of Claims, however, has liberally construed "subject inventions," so as to include within its purview any invention which is "umbilically connnected" to the government-funded research. Thus, the government was deemed to possess a royalty-free license to a potential crash helmet though the motivation therefor was a privately funded research project, where the inventors of the helmet had been simultaneously engaged in government-funded studies on the biological effects of acceleration on the human body. The court reasoned that the crash helmet had been developed through knowledge and experience gained under the government contract.[5.1] An even more extreme case involved the acquisition by purchase by a contractor, after it had completed work on a government contract, of a patent whose claims dominated those of a patent acquired by the government under the contract. Even though, under the express terms of the contract, the government got a license under background patents either owned by the contractor *at the time the contract was entered into or acquired by the contractor before the contract was completed,* it was held that the government acquired the right to practice the invention covered by the claims of its patent, where these claims read on the claims of the contractor's after-acquired dominant patent.[5.2]

[5.1] Mine Safety Appliance Co. v. United States, 364 F.2d 385, 150 U.S.P.Q. 453 (Ct.Cl. 1966).

[5.2] AMP, Inc. v. United States, 389 F.2d 448, 156 U.S.P.Q. 647 (Ct.Cl. 1968).

§ 1[3].   The Atomic Energy Commission

PAGE 172

[*Delete the title of this section and the first text paragraph thereunder, and substitute:*]

[3] Energy Research & Development Administration (ERDA)

In 1974, Congress abolished the Atomic Energy Commission, transferring its functions to the newly created Energy Research & Development Administration (ERDA) and the Nuclear Regulatory Commission (NRC). P.L. - 93 - 438, 88 Stat. 1239, 42 U.S.C. 5814. Under the transitional provisions (42 U.S.C. 5871), a reference to "Commission" in any existing statute may mean either of the two new agencies.

Unless they waive the rights, the Energy Research & Development Administration and the Nuclear Regulatory Commission own the inventions made by their contractors.[6] Section 152 (42 U.S.C. 2182) giving the AEC the right to take title to patents or inventions made by its contractors does not apply retroactively, and so does not affect contracts entered into by the AEC before the effective date of the statute.[6.1]

Compulsory licensing of any patent deemed to be of primary importance in the production or utilization of special nuclear material or atomic energy is provided for in Section 153 (42 U.S.C. 2183). This provision, however, has been construed as not including safety related inventions, such as chemical compounds useful as anti-radiation agents.[6.2]

[6.1] Spevack v. United States, 183 U.S.P.Q. 349 (Ct.Cl. 1974).
[6.2] Piper v. Atomic Energy Commission, 502 F.2d 1393, 183 U.S.P.Q. 235 (C.C.P.A. 1974).

§ 3. Government Access to Privately Owned Patents

PAGE 178

[*Insert between first and second full text paragraphs:*]

This statute further provides:

> . . . the use or manufacture of an invention described in and covered by a patent of the United States by a contractor, a subcontractor, or any person, firm, or corporation for the Government and with the authorization or consent of the

Government, shall be construed as use or manufacture for the United States.

Recovery by a patentee under the foregoing statute is premised on the theory of eminent domain taking under the Fifth Amendment.[23.1] Government use of a patented invention is viewed as an eminent domain taking of a license under the patent and not as a tort.[23.2]

Not every infringement by a government contractor constitutes an authorization or consent that will make the United States liable for damages. Thus, it was held that the United States did not authorize or consent to the infringement of a patent in the performance of a contract that did not require the contractor to use a particular type of equipment either by specifications or by written instructions from the contracting officer. That portion of 32 C.F.R. 102-1 standard authorization and consent clause that provides that the government authorizes and consents to infringement of any patent "embodied in the structure or composition of any article the delivery of which is accepted by the Government" applies to hardware and other goods procured by, and delivered to, the government for its own use, generally through supply contracts, but does not apply to services.[23.3]

Exclusive jurisdiction in an infringement suit against the United States vests in the Court of Claims.[23.4]

[23.1] Tektronix, Inc. v. United States, 188 U.S.P.Q. 25, 28 (Ct.Cl. 1975).

[23.2] Decca, Ltd. v. United States, 191 U.S.P.Q. 439, 448-49 (Ct.Cl. 1976), *modifying on other grounds* 188 U.S.P.Q. 167 (Ct.Cl. 1975).

[23.3] Carrier Corp. v. United States, 534 F.2d 244, 247, 190 U.S.P.Q. 55, 57 (Ct.Cl. 1976). See also, Price v. United States, 190 U.S.P.Q. 177 (Ct.Cl. 1976); Great Plains Bag Corp. v. St. Regis Paper Co., 188 U.S.P.Q. 561, 563 (S.D. Iowa 1975).

[23.4] Great Plains Bag Corp. v. St. Regis Paper Co., N.23.3 *supra.*

[Insert between second and third full text paragraphs:]

Where the government has an indemnity or "hold harmless" agreement with a supplier, the government can have such supplier summoned to intervene as a third party defendant. U.S.Ct.Cl. Rule 41. Dismissal of the suit against the government because the infringing supplier was deemed not to have been acting with authorization or consent of the government does not preclude the patentee from bringing suit against the infringing supplier in an appropriate U.S. district court.[24.1]

[24.1] Price v. United States, 190 U.S.P.Q. 177 (Ct.Cl. 1976).

PAGE 179

[Insert between first and last text paragraphs:]

Where a royalty rate for the patented invention has been established prior to infringement, the Court of Claims generally adopts the same as the measure of reasonable and entire compensation.[29.1] Use by the government of a patented invention even for testing, evaluation, demonstrational or experimental purposes is compensable use by or for the government. However, a patent owner is not entitled to an adjustment in compensation by reason of inflation occurring subsequent to the date of patent infringement.[29.2]

[29.1] Pitcairn v. United States, 188 U.S.P.Q. 35 (Ct.Cl. 1975), citing Marconi Wireless Telegraph Co. v. United States, 53 U.S.P.Q. 246 (Ct.Cl. 1942), *modified* 320 U.S.1, 57 U.S.P.Q. 471 (1943). See also, Tektronix, Inc. v. United States, 188 U.S.P.Q. 25 (Ct.Cl. 1975).

[29.2] Pitcairn v. United States, N.29.1 *supra.*

[Add text at end of the section:]

More recently it has been held that a state agency is liable for damages for patent infringement, even though that state has not expressly consented to be sued, the Eleventh Amendment to the Constitution to the contrary notwithstanding.[31.1]

[31.1] Lemelson v. Ampex Corp., 372 F. Supp. 708, 181 U.S.P.Q. 313 (N.D.Ill. 1974).

Notes

PAGE 180

[Delete text of footnote 22 and substitute:]
Public Citizens, Inc. v. Sampson, 180 U.S.P.Q. 497 (D.C.C. 1974).

[Delete text of footnote 23 and substitute:]
28 U.S.C. 1498.

Chapter 12

PREPARATION OF PATENT APPLICATIONS

PAGE 184

[*In second text line on the page, delete* "(1) A petition or request for a patent, see Rule 61."]

[*In second text paragraph, delete* "The petition, specification, and oath or declaration must be in the English language." *Substitute:*]

The specification and oath or declaration must be in the English language.

§ 1.   The Petition

PAGE 184

[*Delete text of this section* **in its entirety.** *Substitute:*]

A petition formally requesting the grant of letters patent is no longer required.

§ 2.   The Oath or Declaration

PAGE 185

[*In first line of paragraph numbered* "(2)," *add to text after* "for patent":]

or inventor's certificate

[*In third line of paragraph numbered* "(3)," *add to text after* "or patented":]

or made the subject of an inventor's certificate

PAGE 187

[*Delete the form entitled "Declaration, Power of Attorney, and Petition," and substitute form on pages 64 and 65 of this supplement:*]

ATTORNEY'S DOCKET NO. (IF ANY)

DECLARATION
AND POWER OF ATTORNEY
Original Application

As a below named inventor, I declare that the information given herein is true, that I believe that I am the original, first and sole inventor if only one name is listed at 201 below, or a joint inventor if plural inventors are named below at 201–203, of the invention entitled:

which is described and claimed in:

☐ the attached specification or   ☐ the specification in application Serial No. _____ filed _____
(for declaration not accompanying application)

that I do not know and do not believe that the same was ever known or used in the United States of America before my or our invention thereof or patented or described in any printed publication in any country before my or our invention thereof, or more than one year prior to this application, or in public use or on sale in the United States of America more than one year prior to this application, that the invention has not been patented or made the subject of an inventor's certificate issued before the date of this application in any country foreign to the United States of America on an application filed by me or my legal representatives or assigns more than twelve months prior to this application and that no application for patent or inventor's certificate on this invention has been filed by me or my legal representatives or assigns in any country foreign to the United States of America except as identified below.

FOREIGN APPLICATION(S), IF ANY, FILED **WITHIN** 12 MONTHS PRIOR TO THE FILING DATE OF THIS APPLICATION

COUNTRY	APPLICATION NUMBER	DATE OF FILING (day, month, year)	PRIORITY CLAIMED UNDER 35 U.S.C. 119
			YES — NO —
			YES — NO —
ALL FOREIGN APPLICATIONS, IF ANY, FILED **MORE** THAN 12 MONTHS PRIOR TO THE FILING DATE OF THIS APPLICATION			

POWER OF ATTORNEY: As a named inventor, I hereby appoint the following attorney(s) and/or agent(s) to prosecute this application and transact all business in the Patent and Trademark Office connected therewith. *(list name and registration number)*

SEND CORRESPONDENCE TO:

DIRECT TELEPHONE CALLS TO:
(name and telephone number)

	LAST NAME	FIRST NAME	MIDDLE NAME	
201 FULL NAME OF INVENTOR				
RESIDENCE & CITIZENSHIP	CITY	STATE OR FOREIGN COUNTRY	STATE OR COUNTRY	COUNTRY OF CITIZENSHIP
POST OFFICE ADDRESS	POST OFFICE ADDRESS	CITY		ZIP CODE
202 FULL NAME OF INVENTOR	LAST NAME	FIRST NAME	MIDDLE NAME	
RESIDENCE & CITIZENSHIP	CITY	STATE OR FOREIGN COUNTRY	STATE OR COUNTRY	COUNTRY OF CITIZENSHIP
POST OFFICE ADDRESS	POST OFFICE ADDRESS	CITY		ZIP CODE
203 FULL NAME OF INVENTOR	LAST NAME	FIRST NAME	MIDDLE NAME	
RESIDENCE & CITIZENSHIP	CITY	STATE OR FOREIGN COUNTRY	STATE OR COUNTRY	COUNTRY OF CITIZENSHIP
POST OFFICE ADDRESS	POST OFFICE ADDRESS	CITY		ZIP CODE

I further declare that all statements made herein of my own knowledge are true and that all statements made on information and belief are believed to be true; and further that these statements were made with the knowledge that willful false statements and the like so made are punishable by fine or imprisonment, or both, under section 1001 of Title 18 of the United States Code, and that such willful false statements may jeopardize the validity of the application or any patent issuing thereon

SIGNATURE OF INVENTOR 201	SIGNATURE OF INVENTOR 202	SIGNATURE OF INVENTOR 203
DATE	DATE	DATE

FORM PTO-1294 (4-75)

U. S. DEPARTMENT OF COMMERCE
PATENT AND TRADEMARK OFFICE

§ 3. The Drawing

PAGE 189

[*Add new text after last sentence on the page:*]

The Patent Office's acceptance of applications that have only process claims, without drawings, does not warrant the conclusion that such application need not disclose apparatus to perform the process where the apparatus is not conventional. If the practice of the claimed method requires particular apparatus, the application must provide sufficient disclosure of that apparatus if it is not already available.[19.1]

[19.1] *In re* Gunn, 537 F.2d 1123, 190 U.S.P.Q. 402 (C.C.P.A. 1976).

PAGE 190

[*In third text line of first paragraph on the page, add after sentence ending in footnote* **21**:]

Similarly, an error in a patent drawing may make it inadequate as a prior description.[21.1]

[21.1] Hughes Aircraft Co. v. General Instrument Corp., 374 F. Supp. 1166, 1175, 182 U.S.P.Q. 11, 17 (D.Del. 1974).

[*Add after first text paragraph, before text of Rule 83:*]

At least one court, however, has taken the position that no invention can be saved by features that appear only in figures, and are not mentioned in the text of the specification.[22.1]

[22.1] Maclaren v. B-I-W Group, Inc., 535 F.2d 1367, 1373, 190 U.S.P.Q. 513, 517 (2d Cir. 1976).

§ 5. Specification

§ 5[5]. Detailed Description

PAGE 197

[*Add text after sentence numbered "(4)":*]

It does not matter under Section 112, first paragraph, how the specification describes the subject matter later claimed, but it must do so in some way in order to comply with the description-of-the-invention requirement.[30.1] The function of the description requirement is to ensure that the inventor possessed, as of the filing date of the application relied upon, the specific subject matter later claimed by him. It is not necessary that the application describe the claim limitations exactly. The primary consideration is factual and depends on the nature of the invention and the amount of knowledge imparted by the disclosure to those skilled in the art.[30.2]

[30.1] *In re* Mott, 539 F.2d 1291, 1299, 190 U.S.P.Q. 536, 542 (C.C.P.A. 1976).
[30.2] *In re* Wertheim, 541 F.2d 257, 262, 191 U.S.P.Q. 91, 96 (C.C.P.A. 1976).

[Add immediately preceding last paragraph on the page (paragraph running over to page 198):]

The deliberate failure to disclose the "best mode" is grounds for denying a patent or invalidating one already issued.[34.1] Where there was no actual intent to conceal the best mode, failure to have disclosed it completely does not invalidate the patent.[34.2] The patentee need disclose only the best mode he conceived for practicing his invention and not all conceivable modes. To require otherwise would place upon him an unreasonable burden not required by Section 112.[34.3]

More recently the Court of Customs and Patent Appeals has said that a working example is not always necessary and that the specification need be no more specific under Rule 71(b) than is required by the enablement provision of Section 112. The test is whether there is disclosed sufficient working procedure for one skilled in the art to practice the claimed invention without undue experimentation. Relevant considerations in determining whether a disclosure is enabling are: (1) the nature of the invention; (2) the state of the prior art; (3) the relative skill in the art; and (4) the presence or absence of a working example.[34.4] However, this view is not shared by all U.S. district courts. Thus, one United States district judge concluded that accepted practice requires that the specification set forth a specific operative embodiment of the invention.[34.5]

[34.1] Dale Electronics, Inc. v. R.C.L. Electronics, Inc., 488 F.2d 382, 180 U.S.P.Q. 225 (1st Cir. 1973); Reynolds Metals Co. v. Acom Building Components, Inc., — F. Supp. —, 185 U.S.P.Q. 30 (E.D. Mich. 1975); Fred Whitaker Co. v. E.T. Barwick Industries, Inc.,

183 U.S.P.Q. 197 (N.D.Ga. 1974); Mclaren v. B-I-W Group, Inc., 182 U.S.P.Q. 260 (S.D.N.Y. 1974); Ex parte Richter, 185 U.S.P.Q. 38 (P.O.Bd.App. 1974).

34.2 Dow Corning Corp. v. Surgitek, Inc., 378 F. Supp. 1128, 182 U.S.P.Q. 688 (E.D.Wis. 1974).

34.3 Lockheed Aircraft Corp. v. United States, 190 U.S.P.Q. 134, 147 (Ct.Cl. 1976).

34.4 *In re* Stephens, 529 F.2d 1343, 188 U.S.P.Q. 659 (C.C.P.A. 1976).

34.5 Westwood Chemical, Inc. v. Dow Corning Corp., 189 U.S.P.Q. 649, 664-65 (E.D. Mich. 1975).

PAGE 198

[*In fourth text line on the page, add after* "most nearly relates.":]

Although Section 112 requires an exact description of the invention, it does not require description in terms of exact measurements.[35.1] Production specifications are not part of necessary patent disclosure. It is normal practice to retain commercial details of a manufacturing process in confidence.[35.2] An invention does not have to be described in *ipsis verbis* in order to satisfy the description requirement of Section 112.[35.3] There is no requirement that the drawings accompanying a patent be so detailed as to be a production specification.[35.4]

35.1 U.S. Philips Corp. v. National Micronetics, Inc., 410 F. Supp. 449, 455, 188 U.S.P.Q. 662, 667-68 (S.D.N.Y. 1976).

35.2 International Telephone & Telegraph Corp. v. Raychem Corp., — F. Supp. —, 188 U.S.P.Q. 214 (D.Mass. 1975). See also, Douglas v. United States, 387 F. Supp. 1345, 184 U.S.P.Q. 613 (Ct.Cl. 1975).

35.3 Electronic Memories & Magnetics Corp. v. Control Data Corp., 188 U.S.P.Q. 448, 449 (1975).

35.4 Milgo Electronics Corp. v. United Telecommunications, Inc., 189 U.S.P.Q. 160, 168 (D.Kan. 1976).

[*In fourth line of first full text paragraph, add after* "inventive faculties.":]

A patent issued after applicant's filing date cannot be relied upon as evidence to show that applicant's specification is enabling.[36.1]

36.1 *In re* Scarborough, 500 F.2d 560, 182 U.S.P.Q. 298 (C.C.P.A. 1974).

[*Insert between first and second full text paragraphs:*]

Some experimentation to select operating parameters is permissible.[37.1] A patent, however, is not an invitation to experiment in order to determine the invention.[37.2] The specification need not teach that which is known and obvious to those skilled in the art.[37.3]

[37.1] *In re* Angstadt, 537 F.2d 498, 502, 190 U.S.P.Q. 214, 218 (C.C.P.A. 1976); *In re* Geerdes, 491 F.2d 1260, 1265, 180 U.S.P.Q. 789, 793 (C.C.P.A. 1974); Columbia Broadcasting System, Inc. v. Zenith Radio Corp., 185 U.S.P.Q. 662, 670 (N.D.Ill. 1975).

[37.2] Westwood Chemical, Inc. v. Dow Corning Corp., — F. Supp. —, 189 U.S.P.Q. 649, 665 (E.D. Mich. 1975).

[37.3] National Research Development Corp. v. Great Lakes Carbon Corp., 410 F. Supp. 1108, 1124, 188 U.S.P.Q. 327, 339-40 (D.Del. 1975).

PAGE 199

[Add text after first paragraph on the page:]

It has been said that an inventor may be his own lexicographer in describing his invention.[39.1] However, no term may be given a meaning that is repugnant to the usual meaning of the term. M.P.E.P. 608.01(o). Moreover, the Patent Office and Court of Customs & Patent Appeals do not look with favor upon the adoption by an applicant of new legal terminology, absent some compelling reason.[39.2]

There are four instances in which the description-of-the-invention requirement was held to have been satisfied notwithstanding the absence of an explicit description:

(1) Where the description was in the original claims;

(2) Where the description incorporated other information by reference;

(3) Where the broad scope was deemed implicit to those skilled in the art; and

(4) Where the description was deemed inherent.

To illustrate,

(1) Unamended, original claims are deemed part of the description of the invention.[39.3] When subject matter not shown in the drawing or described in the specification is claimed in the case as filed, the description of the invention and drawing should be amended to show this subject matter. M.P.E.P. 608.01(e).

(2) An application for a patent when filed may incorporate "essential material" by reference to (1) a United States patent, or (2) an allowed U.S. application.[39.4] "Essential material" may not be incorporated by reference to (a) patents issued by foreign countries, to (b) nonpatent publications, to (c) a patent or application which itself

incorporates "essential material" by reference, or to (d) a foreign application.[39.5]

Nonessential subject matter may be incorporated by reference to (a) patents issued by the United States or foreign countries, (b) prior filed, commonly owned U.S. applications, or (c) nonpatent publications, for purposes of indicating the background of the invention or illustrating the state of the art. M.P.E.P. 608.01(p). Even nonessential subject matter may not be incorporated by reference to a pending application unless the application is co-owned.[39.6] A mere reference to an earlier application does not automatically incorporate by reference all disclosure of the earlier application. There must be an incorporating statement which clearly identifies the subject matter which is incorporated.[39.7] The Commissioner is visited with broad discretion to determine in what instances mere incorporation by reference is proper and in what instances the material incorporated must be added to the disclosure.[39.8]

(3) Claimed subject matter need not be described in haec verba in the specification in order for the specification to satisfy the description-of-the-invention requirement.[39.9]

(4) By disclosing in a patent application structure that inherently performs a function, operates according to a theory, or has an advantage, the applicant necessarily discloses that function, theory, or advantage even though he says nothing concerning it, and the application may later be amended to recite the function, theory, or advantage without introducing new matter.[39.10]

[39.1] Chicago Foundry Co. v. Burnside Foundry Co., 132 F.2d 812, 814, 56 U.S.P.Q. 283, 286 (7th Cir. 1943).

[39.2] In re Mott, 539 F.2d 1291, 1295, 190 U.S.P.Q. 536, 540 (C.C.P.A. 1976).

[39.3] General Electric Co. v. United States, 191 U.S.P.Q. 594, 604-05 (Ct.Cl. 1976); In re Bowen, 492 F.2d 859, 864, 181 U.S.P.Q. 48, 52 (C.C.P.A. 1974); In re Gardiner, 475 F.2d 1389, 1391 177 U.S.P.Q. 396, 397 (C.C.P.A. 1973), aff'd on reconsideration 480 F.2d 879, 178 U.S.P.Q. 149 (C.C.P.A. 1973); In re Anderson, 471 F.2d 1237, 1238, 176 U.S.P.Q. 331, 332 (C.C.P.A. 1972).

[39.4] Lundy Electronics, Inc. v. Optical Systems, Inc., 362 F. Supp. 130, 154, 178 U.S.P.Q. 525, 543 (E.D.Va. 1973), aff'd 493 F.2d 1222 (4th Cir. 1974); General Electric Co. v. Brenner, 407 F.2d 1258, 1262-63, 159 U.S.P.Q. 335, 338 (D.C.C. 1968).

[39.5] In re Hawkins (II), 486 F.2d 579, 179 U.S.P.Q. 163 (C.C.P.A. 1973) (co-pending British application); In re Henecke, 486 F.2d 582, 179 U.S.P.Q. 166 (C.C.P.A. 1973) (co-pending German application).

[39.6] Westwood Chemical, Inc. v. Dow Corning Corp., 189 U.S.P.Q. 649, 660 (E.D.Mich. 1975).

[39.7] In re Glass, 492 F.2d 1228, 181 U.S.P.Q. 31 (C.C.P.A. 1974); Ex parte Hageman, 179 U.S.P.Q. 747 (P.O.Bd.App. 1972).

39.8 *In re* Hawkins (I), 486 F.2d 569, 179 U.S.P.Q. 157, 162 (C.C.P.A. 1973); *In re* Hawkins (III), 486 F.2d 577, 179 U.S.P.Q. 167 (C.C.P.A. 1973).

39.9 *In re* Smith, 481 F.2d 910, 914, 178 U.S.P.Q. 620, 624 (C.C.P.A. 1973).

39.10 *In re* Smythe, 480 F.2d 1376, 1385, 178 U.S.P.Q. 279, 285 (C.C.P.A. 1973).

PAGE 200

[Delete last text paragraph in § 1[5] and substitute:]

It has been held improper, however, for an examiner to reject a claim drawn to a genus on the ground that it does not properly define his invention.[46] Section 112, second paragraph, allows an applicant to claim whatever he regards as his invention. And an applicant can *change* the subject matter which he regards as his invention.[46.1] It has also been held improper to reject a claim drawn to a genus where the sole basis therefor is merely that the examiner is of the opinion that there is an insufficient number of working examples disclosed to support a generic claim. There is no requirement that all compositions that may work be specifically disclosed in the patent specification.[46.2]

Mention of representative compounds encompassed by generic claim language clearly is not required by Section 112 or any other portion of the statute.[47] There must be, however, a reasonable correlation between the scope of the disclosure and the scope of the claim.[47.1] Such correlation may be taught either expressly, inherently, or implicitly.[47.2] Once such correlation is taught, the burden shifts to the Patent & Trademark Office to back up with acceptable evidence or reasoning its assertion that the scope of enablement is not commensurate with the scope of the protection sought.[47.3] An applicant must be given an opportunity to cite or to present other evidence in rebuttal.[47.4] That a claim is readable on inoperative embodiments, because values of operating conditions are not recited therein, is an insufficient basis for rejecting such claim, where the selection of values of conditions which would render the claim operable would be obvious to a person of ordinary skill in the art.[48]

Where an applicant has broad claims, but equally broad language in the specification, and there is no reason to expect any inoperative species is being covered, there is full compliance with the description-of-the-invention requirement.[48.1] The scope of the enablement provided to one of ordinary skill in the art must be commensurate with the scope of the protection sought by the claims.

The scope of the enablement varies inversely with the degree of unpredictability involved. Although disclosure of every species encompassed by a claim is not required, even in unpredictable arts, each case must be determined on its own facts in determining the adequacy of Section 112 disclosure.[46.2] The peculiar degree of unpredictability associated with the catalysis art does not translate into a requirement that an enabling disclosure provide an exhaustive listing of all possible treating steps and agents that would be efficacious.[46.3] A disclosure may be so lacking in enablement as to be incapable of supporting any claim.[46.4]

[46] *In re* Borkowski, 422 F.2d 904, 164 U.S.P.Q. 642 (C.C.P.A. 1970; *In re* Wakefield, 422 F.2d 897, 164 U.S.P.Q. 636 (C.C.P.A. 1970).

[46.1] Scandiamant Aktiebolag v. Commissioner, 509 F.2d 463, 470, 184 U.S.P.Q. 201, 206 (D.C.C. 1974).

[46.2] Armstrong Cork Co. v. Congoleum Industries, Inc., 399 F. Supp. 1141, 1152, 188 U.S.P.Q. 679, 688 (E.D.Pa. 1975).

[47] *In re* Robins, 429 F.2d 452, 166 U.S.P.Q. 552 (C.C.P.A. 1970).

[47.1] *In re* Bowen, 492 F.2d 859, 181 U.S.P.Q. 48 (C.C.P.A. 1974); Ex parte Richter, 185 U.S.P.Q. 38 (P.O.Bd.App. 1974).

[47.2] Bloch v. Sze, 484 F.2d 1202, 179 U.S.P.Q. 374 (C.C.P.A. 1973).

[47.3] *In re* Dinh-Nguyen, 492 F.2d 856, 181 U.S.P.Q. 46 (C.C.P.A. 1974); *In re* Mayhew, 481 F.2d 1373, 179 U.S.P.Q. 42 (C.C.P.A. 1973).

[47.4] *In re* Eynde, 480 F.2d 1364, 178 U.S.P.Q. 470 (C.C.P.A. 1973); Ex parte Hageman, 179 U.S.P.Q. 747 (P.O.Bd.App. 1972).

[48] *In re* Skrivan, 427 F.2d 801, 166 U.S.P.Q. 85 (C.C.P.A. 1970).

[48.1] Ex parte Altermatt, 183 U.S.P.Q. 436 (P.O.Bd.App. 1974).

[48.2] *In re* Angstadt, 537 F.2d 498, 190 U.S.P.Q. 214 (C.C.P.A. 1976).

[48.3] Ex parte Volheim, 191 U.S.P.Q. 407 (P.O.Bd.App. 1976).

[48.4] *In re* Knowlton, 500 F.2d 566, 183 U.S.P.Q. 33 (C.C.P.A. 1974).

§ 5[6]. The Claims

PAGE 200

[*In fifth text line of first paragraph of this section, add after sentence ending in footnote* 49:]

While these two functions would appear to correspond to the specification and claims respectively, at least one United States district court has taken the position that the *claims* embody sufficient specificity to permit persons skilled in the art to understand and practice the claim's teachings.[49.1]

[49.1] St. Regis Paper Co. v. Benus Co., 403 F. Supp. 776, 787, 188 U.S.P.Q. 107, 117 (S.D.Ill. 1975).

PAGE 201

[Add text after quotation from Section 112:]

A claim that incorporates all elements of another claim is a dependent claim.[50.1]

[50.1] Faulkner v. Baldwin Piano & Organ Co., 189 U.S.P.Q. 695, 706 (N.D.Ill. 1976).

§ 5[6][b]. Antecedent basis must be present

PAGE 202

[At end of first text paragraph in the section, add footnote 50.2 to "recitation.":]

[50.2] *In re* Mercier, 515 F.2d 1161, 1168, 185 U.S.P.Q. 774, 780 (C.C.P.A. 1975).

PAGE 203

[Add text after end of the "Illustration," carried over from page 202:]

It has been held that the claim language "a document in cylindrical shape" provides sufficient antecedent basis to support the limitation "elements of the *cylinder.*"[51.1]

[51.1] Ex parte Shepard, 188 U.S.P.Q. 536, 539 (P.O.Bd.App. 1974).

§ 5[6][d]. Alternative expressions are normally not permitted

PAGE 203

[In fourth text line in this section, add after sentence ending in footnote 53:]

Nevertheless, the use of "and/or" on occasion has been at least implicitly approved.[53.1]

[53.1] *In re* Rice, 481 F.2d 1316, 178 U.S.P.Q. 478 (C.C.P.A. 1973).

PAGE 203

[Add new sections: §§ 5[6][e]-5[6][k].]

[e] "Substantially"

The use of the qualifying adverb "substantially" has been sanctioned in various contexts. Its purpose is to prevent avoidance of literal infringement by minor changes that do not cause loss of an invention's benefit.[55] Its use is not indefinite as a matter of law.[56] The terminology "substantially the same diameter" was at least in one context deemed to allow for a 15° taper.[57]

The use of "substantially increase" has been deemed to satisfy the definiteness requirement of 35 U.S.C. 112, second paragraph.[58]

[f] "About"

A court declined to hold that "about 1.2-1.8" would necessarily exclude less than 1.0.[59]

[g] "Generally"

The phrase "generally planar reflective surface" was not deemed indefinite, being construed to allow for irregular deviations from a perfectly flat surface and not to encompass distinctly arcuate surfaces.[60]

[h] Relative terminology

If the language of the claims is not so indefinite as to defeat the purposes of the statutory requirement of precision, claims will be validated even when seemingly vague, as including such words as "high" or "slight excess." The test is whether claims, read in context of the particular case, meet a suitable standard of precision—a standard which varies from case to case. Objectionable indefiniteness is determined by the facts in each case and not by reference to an abstract rule.[61]

[i] Magnitudes in functional terms

A magnitude expressed in terms of the desired result rather than in absolute number is not necessarily indefinite. Accordingly, the use of the terminology "an effective amount" has been deemed proper where such terminology was qualified by the function which is to be achieved.[62]

[j] Ranges and proportions

A composition claim which recites each component as a range is not indefinite where components would together total more than 100% if the maximum amount of one range were selected together with the minimum amounts of the range specified for the remaining components.[63]

The failure to specify a lower limit for a range is not necessarily indefinite.[64]

[k] Miscellaneous

The recitation in a claim of "a cylindrical surface" was deemed *not* to read on an "arcuate support" of a prior art reference.[65]

[55] National Research Development Corp. v. Great Lakes Carbon Corp., 410 F. Supp. 1108, 1116, 188 U.S.P.Q. 327, 333 (D.Del. 1975).

[56] U.S. Philips Corp. v. National Micronetics, Inc., 410 F. Supp. 449, 455, 188 U.S.P.Q. 662, 668 (S.D.N.Y. 1976).

[57] Olympic Fastening Systems, Inc. v. Textron, Inc., 504 F.2d 609, 618, 183 U.S.P.Q. 449, 455 (6th Cir. 1974), *cert. denied* 420 U.S. 1004 (1975).

[58] *In re* Mattison, 509 F.2d 563, 564, 184 U.S.P.Q. 484, 486 (C.C.P.A. 1974).

[59] Johnson & Johnson v. W.L. Gore & Associates, Inc., — F. Supp. —, 181 U.S.P.Q. 597, 598 (D.Del. 1974).

[60] Arvin Industries, Inc. v. Berns Air King Corp., 525 F.2d 182, 185, 188 U.S.P.Q. 49, 51 (7th Cir. 1975).

[61] Charvat v. Commissioner, 503 F.2d 138, 148-49, 182 U.S.P.Q. 577, 585-86 (D.C.C. 1974).

[62] *In re* Watson, 517 F.2d 465, 477, 186 U.S.P.Q. 11, 20 (C.C.P.A. 1975).

[63] *In re* Kroekel, 504 F.2d 1143, 1146, 183 U.S.P.Q. 610, 611 (C.C.P.A. 1974).

[64] *In re* Kirsch, 498 F.2d 1389, 1393-94, 182 U.S.P.Q. 286, 290 (C.C.P.A. 1974).

[65] Ex parte Shepard, 188 U.S.P.Q. 536, 538 (P.O.Bd.App. 1974).

§ 5[7]. Signature

PAGE 203

[*Add new text at end of the section:*]

An attorney can sign on behalf of a corporate assignee an exclusive licensee, or a trustee in bankruptcy, but cannot sign on behalf of an individual inventor unless there were some other bases of asserting "sufficient proprietary interest."[66]

Under Section 118:

> Whenever an inventor refuses to execute an application for patent, or cannot be found or reached after a diligent effort, a person to whom the inventor has assigned or agreed in writing to assign the invention or who otherwise shows sufficient proprietary interest in the matter justifying such action, may

make application for patent on behalf of and as agent for the inventor on proof of the pertinent facts and a showing that such action is necessary to preserve the rights of the parties or to prevent irreparable damage; and the Commissioner may grant a patent to such inventor upon such notice to him as the Commissioner deems sufficient, and on compliance with such regulations as he prescribes.

Section 118 has been construed as *not* sanctioning the signing of an application by the attorney or agent of the applicant, even where such action was ratified by the applicant. The only person authorized under Title 35 to make application for patent on behalf of joint inventors, other than one of the joint inventors (35 U.S.C. 116) or the legal representative of deceased or incapacitated inventors (35 U.S.C. 117) is a person to whom the inventor has assigned or agreed in writing to assign the invention or who otherwise shows sufficient proprietary interest in the matter justifying such action (35 U.S.C. 118). A "proprietary" interest at the very least suggests some element of ownership or dominion.[67]

[66] *In re* Striker, 182 U.S.P.Q. 507 (P.O.Sol. 1973).
[67] Staeger v. Comm'r, 189 U.S.P.Q. 272, 274 (D.D.C. 1976).

Notes

PAGE 204

[*Add to footnote* 37:]

Milgo Electronics Corp. v. United Telecommunications, Inc., 189 U.S.P.Q. 160, 168 (D.Kan. 1976).

[*Add to footnote* 38:]

Armstrong Cork Co. v. Congoleum Industries, Inc., 399 F. Supp. 1141, 1152, 188 U.S.P.Q. 679, 688 (E.D.Pa. 1975).

PAGE 205

[*Add to footnote* 49:]

International Telephone & Telegraph Corp. v. Raychem Corp., 538 F.2d 453, 460, 191 U.S.P.Q. 1, 7 (1st Cir. 1976); Westwood Chemical, Inc., 189 U.S.P.Q. 649, 659 (E.D.Mich. 1975).

Chapter 13

PROSECUTING PATENT APPLICATIONS

PAGE 209

[In third text line on the page, add after "Department."*:]*

Congress amended title 35 of the United States Code to change the name of the Patent Office to the "Patent & Trademark Office." Act of January 2, 1975, Pub. L. 93-596, 88 Stat. 1949.[a1]

[a1] See Standard Oil Co. v. Montedison, S.P.A., 540 F.2d 611, 613, 191 U.S.P.Q. 657, 658 (3d Cir. 1976).

§ 1. The Patent Bar

PAGE 210

[Insert between second and third full text paragraphs:]

While Rule 341(b) appears to limit registration of patent agents to United States citizens, the Patent office will recognize as patent agents otherwise qualified non-lawyer aliens when the alien is (1) domiciled or resides in the United States while being employed in the patent department of a corporation or by a law firm composed of registered patent attorneys and (2) the alien is classified as a "permanent resident" by the Attorney General. And this will be the case whether or not the country of which he is a citizen accords substantially reciprocal privileges to U.S. citizens.[8.1] However, the recognition of an alien as a patent agent will remain in force only so long as he resides or remains domiciled in the United States.[8.2]

[8.1] *In re* Gresset, 187 U.S.P.Q. 351 (Comm.Pat. 1976); *In re* Messulam, 185 U.S.P.Q. 438 (Comm.Pat. 1975); *In re* Bramham, 181 U.S.P.Q. 723 (Comm.Pat. 1974); *In re* Jackson, 181 U.S.P.Q. 724 (Comm.Pat. 1974).
[8.2] *In re* Bhogarajn, 178 U.S.P.Q. 628 (Comm.Pat. 1973).

PAGE 210

[In third full text paragraph, add after "not more than $1,000."*:]*

While violation of Section 33 may give rise to a civil cause of action cognizable in the federal courts, Section 33 has been deemed as not an act "relating to patents" within the meaning of 28 U.S.C. 1338. Therefore, the amount in controversy must exceed the sum or value of $10,000 within the meaning of 28 U.S.C. 1331(a).[8.3] The damage suffered by each member of a class whose suit is based upon jurisdiction under 28 U.S.C. 1331(a) must satisfy the jurisdictional amount prescribed in 28 U.S.C. 1331(a), that is, damages may not be aggregated by the members of the class to reach the threshold jurisdictional amount.[8.4]

[8.3] Enders v. American Patent Search Co., 535 F.2d 1085, 1088, 189 U.S.P.Q. 569 (9th Cir. 1976).
[8.4] Zahn v. International Paper Co., 414 U.S. 291, 301 (1973).

PAGE 211

[*Add at end of text paragraph which follows quotation at top of page:*]

However, this view is by no means universal.[11.1] Some courts have taken the position that the attorney work product privilege does not extend to ex parte patent prosecution.[11.2] Other courts appear to extend the work product privilege to patent prosecution.[11.3]

At least one court has taken the position that the attorney work product privilege does not extend to ex parte patent prosecution.[11.4]

[11.1] Burlington Industries v. Exxon Corp., 65 F.R.D. 26, 40, 184 U.S.P.Q. 651, 657 (D.Md. 1974).
[11.2] Electronic Memories & Magnetics Corp. v. Control Data Corp., — F. Supp. —, —, 188 U.S.P.Q. 449, 450 (N.D.Ill. 1975).
[11.3] Duplan Corp. v. Deering Milliken, Inc., 184 U.S.P.Q. 775, 786 (D.S.C. 1975); Schenectady Chemicals, Inc. v. General Electric Co., 184 U.S.P.Q. 208, 209 (N.D.N.Y. 1974).
[11.4] Electronic Memories & Magnetics Corp. v. Control Data Corp., 188 U.S.P.Q. 449, 450 (N.D.Ill. 1975).

§ 2.   Filing the Patent Application

PAGE 212

[*Delete list numbered "(1)" to "(5)" at top of page, and substitute:*]

(1) A specification, including a claim or claims, see Rules 71-77.
(2) An oath or declaration, see Rule 65.
(3) Drawings, when necessary, see Rules 81-88.
(4) The prescribed filing fee, see Rule 21.

§ 1[3]. Continuing Applications and Res Judicata

PAGE 214

*[Immediately following text paragraph ending in footnote **14**, add:]*

The Patent & Trademark Office, however, does not look with favor on an applicant who files a series of continuation-in-part applications to avoid divulging a basic patentable invention. Under such circumstances a rejection based on laches will *not* be sustained, absent a prior warning in the preceding application that filing future applications in a series without permitting the present one to issue may result in a sustainable rejection based on his conduct, which is contrary to the purpose of the Constitution and the patent laws.[14.1]

[14.1] Ex parte Hull, 191 U.S.P.Q. 157 (P.O.Bd.App. 1975).

§ 1[3][b]. Continuation-in-part

PAGE 215

*[Add footnote **19.1** at end of last sentence on the page (after the word, "application.").]*

[19.1] Kaz Manufacturing Co. v. Northern Electric Co., 189 U.S.P.Q. 464, 478 (S.D.N.Y. 1976).

§ 1[3][d]. Res judicata

PAGE 218

*[In 14th text line of paragraph carried over from page 217, add after sentence ending in footnote **29**:]*

There is a question as to whether an unappealed Board of Appeals decision affirming the examiner's rejection on the ground of res judicata is sufficient to permit the Patent Office to reject even identical claims in a continuation application solely on the ground of res judicata.[29.1] While res judicata has its proper place in the law as a reflection of a policy invoked to settle disputes and put an end to litigation, the prosecution of patent applications is not exactly either a dispute or litigation in the usual sense of these terms. There are additional public policy considerations which have a bearing here, namely, furtherance of the policy inherent in the patent laws to grant patents when the Patent Office finds that *patentable* inventions have been disclosed and properly claimed so that such inventions are made public through the grant. The granting of such patents is also in the public interest in that it may stimulate the commercialization of the patented invention.[29.2]

[29.1] The Plastic Contact Lens Co. v. Gottschalk, 484 F.2d 837, 179 U.S.P.Q. 262 (D.C.C. 1973), *rev'g* Plastic Contact Lens Co. v. Schulyer, 334 F. Supp. 464, 172 U.S.P.Q. 97 (D.C.C. 1971).
[29.2] *In re* Craig, 411 F.2d 1333, 1335-36, 162 U.S.P.Q. 157, 159 (C.C.P.A. 1969).

§ 3. Outline of Ex Parte Prosecution

PAGE 218

[*In ninth text line of first paragraph in this section, add footnote* **32.1** *after* "applicant or owner.":]

[32.1] Sears v. Gottschalk, 502 F.2d 122, 183 U.S.P.Q. 134 (4th Cir. 1974).

[*Add new text after new footnote* **32.1**:]

Public Use Proceedings are not within Section 122 and implementing Rule 14. Access to petition instituting such proceeding and related papers, which are retained in a file separate from patent's file wrapper history, is not part of Rule 11(a). A petition for access to the record of a public use proceeding is treated under Rule 182 as a case not specifically provided for.[32.2]

An exception to this rule exists in regard to a reissue application for a patent involved in litigation.[32.3] The Sunshine Act amendment to 5 U.S.C. 552(b)(3) has been held not to open the files of patent applications to public scrutiny. However, Patent & Trademark Office manuscript decisions, by virtue of the Freedom of Information Act, 5 U.S.C. 552 et seq., are open to public scrutiny.

[32.2] *In re* Public Use Proceeding Bourne, 191 U.S.P.Q. 255 (P.O.Solicitor 1976).
[32.3] International Paper Co. v. Fiberboard Corp., 181 U.S.P.Q. 740, 742 (D.Del. 1974).
[32.4] Irons v. Gottschalk, — F.2d —, 191 U.S.P.Q. 481 (D.C.C. 1976).

PAGE 219

[In second text line of first full paragraph on the page, add after "known as the file wrapper.":]

The file wrapper has been defined as the written record of preliminary negotiations between the applicant and the Patent & Trademark Office for patent monopoly contract.[34.1]

[34.1] Norton Company v. Carborundum Co., 530 F.2d 435, 440, 189 U.S.P.Q. 1, 5 (1st Cir. 1976).

§ 3[1]. Action Taken by the Examiner

PAGE 220

[Add after second full text paragraph:]

The Commissioner may delegate authority to review petitions addressed to him. While the Commissioner may personally review decisions of officials having delegated authority to render a decision, such review is within the sound discretion of the Commissioner and is not a matter of right.[35.1]

[35.1] *In re* Staeger, 189 U.S.P.Q. 284 (Comm.Pat. 1974).

[Add at end of third full text paragraph:]

Claims not included in any rejection would seem allowable.[35.2]

[35.2] Ex parte Gastambide, 189 U.S.P.Q. 643 (P.O.Bd.App. 1974).

PAGE 221

[Add text after last sentence in this section:]

The principal consequence of a Quayle Action is that its issuance closes further prosecution on the merits, so that additional claims may no longer be introduced into the case.[36.1]

[36.1] Ex parte Quayle, 1935 C.D. 11, 4530.G. 213 (Comm.Pat. 1935).

§ 3[2]. Response by Applicant

PAGE 221

[*In sixth text line of second paragraph of the section, add footnote* **36.2** *after* "his case.".:]

[36.2] Pfizer, Inc. v. International Rectifier Corp., 538 F.2d 180, 193, 190 U.S.P.Q. 273, 284 (8th Cir. 1976), citing PATENT LAW FUNDAMENTALS as authority.

§ 4. Appellate Review

§ 4[1]. By the Patent Office Board of Appeals

PAGE 229

[*In fifth text line of first full paragraph, add after* "for so holding.".:]

The ultimate criterion of whether a rejection is "new" in a Board of Appeals' decision is whether the applicant had a fair opportunity to react to the thrust of the rejection, for otherwise he could be deprived of administrative due process rights.[66.1]

[66.1] *In re* Kronig, 539 F.2d 1300, 1302-03, 190 U.S.P.Q. 425 (C.C.P.A. 1976).

[*Add after first full text paragraph:*]

Where the Board of Appeals makes a new ground of rejection pursuant to Rule 196(6) and : (1) the applicant elects to seek further consideration before the Primary Examiner, a shortened statutory period for responding to the Board's new ground of rejection is set to expire *30 days* from the date of its decision; (2) the applicant elects to seek review under Sections 141 and 145 with respect to the affirmed rejection, the effective date of the affirmance is deferred until conclusion of the prosecution before the examiner unless, as a mere incident to the limited prosecution, the affirmed rejection is overcome.[67.1] Ex parte decisions by the Board of Appeals are not controlling on issues to be decided by the Board of Patent Interferences.[67.2]

[67.1] Ex parte Mott, 190 U.S.P.Q. 311, 316 (P.O.Bd.App. 1975).

[67.2] Wetmore v. Quick, 536 F.2d 937, 942, 190 U.S.P.Q. 223, 228 (C.C.P.A. 1976).

[In second text line of second full paragraph, add footnote 67.3 after "allow a case.":]

[67.3] Palmer v. Dudziki, 481 F.2d 1377, 1387, 178 U.S.P.Q. 609, 616 (C.C.P.A. 1973).

[In fourth text line of last paragraph (on page 229), delete "are appointed by, and serve at the pleasure of, the President;" and substitute:]

shall be appointed under the classified civil service P.L. 93-596, sec. 1, 88 Stat. 1949 (January 2, 1975); P.L. 93-601, sec. 2, 88 Stat. 1956 (January 2, 1975).

[In ninth text line of last paragraph, add after "Commissioner of Patents":]

, the deputy commissioner,

§ 4[2]. Court Review

PAGE 230

[In fourth text line of first paragraph on the page, add after "against the applicant.":]

Even the proceeding before the Patent Office Board of Appeals is not deemed to be of an adversarial nature.[70.1]

[70.1] W.L. Gore & Associates, Inc. v. Carlisle Corp., 381 F. Supp. 680, 691, 183 U.S.P.Q. 459, 466 (D.Del. 1974).

[Insert text between first and second paragraphs:]

The action by the Board of Appeals must amount to a "decision," otherwise neither the Court of Customs & Patent Appeals nor the District Court for the District of Columbia will have jurisdiction to review the action. Accordingly, it has been held that mere comment made by the Board of Appeals to the effect that the examiner might wish to review his allowance of claims in light of the Board's holding did not amount to a "decision" subject to review of the Court of Customs & Patent Appeals.[70.2]

[70.2] *In re* Loehr, 500 F.2d 1390, 1394, 183 U.S.P.Q. 56, 59 (C.C.P.A. 1974).

[In fifth text line of last paragraph on the page (paragraph running over to page 231), add after "into the record.":]

The Court of Customs & Patent Appeals has no jurisdiction with respect to the claims that were allowed by the Primary Examiner and not subject to Board of Appeals decision.[76.1] The Court of Customs & Patent Appeals does have jurisdiction to consider a petition for a writ of mandamus.[76.2]

[76.1] *In re* Hayashibara, 525 F.2d 1062, 1066, 188 U.S.P.Q. 4, 6 (C.C.P.A. 1975).
[76.2] Seng v. Dann, 542 F.2d 568, 191 U.S.P.Q. 432 (C.C.P.A. 1976).

PAGE 231

[In first text line on the page, add after sentence ending in footnote 78:]

A mere preponderance of evidence is not enough to justify reversing the Patent & Trademark Office.[78.1]

[78.1] Anderson v. Anderson, 403 F. Supp. 834, 845, 188 U.S.P.Q. 194, 202 (D.D.C. 1975).

[Add text after first full paragraph:]

While neither the United States Court of Appeals for the District of Columbia Circuit nor the District Court for the District of Columbia is bound by the decisions of the Court of Customs & Patent Appeals, the decisions of the latter should be given great weight and treated with respect.[82.1]

[82.1] The Plastic Contact Lens Co. v. Gottschalk, 484 F.2d 837, 839, 179 U.S.P.Q. 262, 264 (D.C.C. 1973); Kollsman v. Ladd, 226 F. Supp. 186, 188, 140 U.S.P.Q. 309, 310-11 (D.D.C. 1964); General Tire and Rubber Co. v. Watson, 184 F. Supp. 344, 350, 125 U.S.P.Q. 628, 632-33 (D.D.C. 1960).

[In fourth text line of second full paragraph, add after "for a writ of certiorari.":]

If a writ of certiorari is not applied for, an appealed application in which no claims are allowed goes "abandoned" when the mandate of the Court of Customs & Patent Appeals affirming the decision of the Patent & Trademark Office is received in the Patent & Trademark Office. Thereafter there exists no application on which a continuing application can be based.[83.1]

[83.1] *In re* Willis, 537 F.2d 513, 190 U.S.P.Q. 327 (C.C.P.A. 1976).

[*Insert text between second and third full paragraphs:*]

Law announced in decisions of the Supreme Court, though in appeals in infringement suits, are applicable by analogy in Patent Office proceedings and must be followed.[84.1]

[84.1] Ex parte Varga, 189 U.S.P.Q. 204, 207 (P.O.Bd.App. 1973).

[*Add text at end of last sentence on the page:*]

The Court of Customs & Patent Appeals has no authority to award attorney's fees.[85.1]

[85.1] Reddy v. Dann, 529 F.2d 1347, 1348, 188 U.S.P.Q. 644, 645 (C.C.P.A. 1976).

§ 5.   Restriction and Double Patenting

PAGE 233

[*In second text line on the page, add footnote* **88.1** *after* "in one application."*:*]

[88.1] Faulkner v. Baldwin Piano & Organ Co., 189 U.S.P.Q. 695, 726 (N.D.Ill. 1976).

PAGE 234

[*In paragraph numbered* "(3)(a)", *add footnote* **95.1** *after* "or by hand,"*:*]

[95.1] General Staple Co. v. Magnifico, 189 U.S.P.Q. 679, 687 (S.D.N.Y. 1976).

§ 6.   Rejections

PAGE 237

[*In eighth text line on the page (in paragraph carried over from page 236), add text after* "examiner's position."*:*]

The examiner has the initial duty of supplying the factual basis for his rejection. He may not, because he may doubt that the invention is patentable, resort to speculation, unfounded assumptions or hindsight reconstruction to supply deficiencies in the factual basis of his rejection.[119.1]

[119.1] *In re* Warner, 379 F.2d 1011, 1017, 154 U.S.P.Q. 173, 178 (C.C.P.A. 1967).

[*Add immediately before first full text paragraph on the page:*]

Moreover, in ex parte prosecution, it should be determined whether the same or similar claims, or obvious claims, were allowed to others.[120.1]

[120.1] *In re* Wertheim, 541 F.2d 257, 264, 191 U.S.P.Q. 90, 97 (C.C.P.A. 1976) (same or similar claims); *In re* Giolito, 530 F.2d 397, 400, 188 U.S.P.Q. 645, 648 (C.C.P.A. 1976).

[*At end of second full text paragraph, add footnote* **120.2** *after the words,* "double patenting.":]

[120.2] Ex parte Haas, 188 U.S.P.Q. 374, 376-77 (P.O.Bd.App. 1975).

[*Add new text at end of the section, following sentence ending in footnote* **122**:]

Prior art references are *evidence* upon which rejections for lack of novelty and obviousness are based.[122.1]

What may be cited as a reference under 35 U.S.C. 103 does not always coincide with what may be applied under 35 U.S.C. 102. For example, a drawing made in a foreign country before patent owner's invention date, while held inadmissible under 35 U.S.C. 102, was held admissible under 35 U.S.C. 103 to prove obviousness. In the same case a patent whose application was filed one day after the patent owner's inventon date was deemed available as a prior art reference with respect to obviousness.[122.2] However, the Court of Customs & Patent Appeals has held that a patent whose application was filed on the same day as appellant's application could not be taken as evidence of the level of skill in the art on the day appellant filed his application but only as evidence of the level of skill of that patentee.[122.3]

[122.1] *In re* Carreira, 532 F.2d 1356, 1358, 189 U.S.P.Q. 461, 463 (C.C.P.A. 1976).
[122.2] Satco, Inc. v. Transequip, Inc., 191 U.S.P.Q. 253 (C.D.Cal. 1975).
[122.3] *In re* Gunn, 537 F.2d 1123, 190 U.S.P.Q. 402 (C.C.P.A. 1976).

§ 6[2]. Under 35 U.S.C. 103

PAGE 238

[In third text line of this section, add after "one or more references.":]

A rejection under 35 U.S.C. 103 may be proper even where the only prior art is the state of the art as admitted by the applicant.[126.1] However, absent such admission, an applicant's disclosure may not be used against him.[126.2]

[126.1] *In re* Ryan, 480 F.2d 1388, 1391, 178 U.S.P.Q. 480 (C.C.P.A. 1973).
[126.2] *In re* Wertheim, 541 F.2d 257, 269, 191 U.S.P.Q. 90, 102 (C.C.P.A. 1976).

PAGE 239

[Add text after paragraph ending in footnote 130:]

The contention that a time lapse of twenty-six years between the two references used in a combination rejection under Section 103 indicates nonobviousness was held unpersuasive absent a showing that that time interval was significant.[130.1]

[130.1] *In re* Deters, 515 F.2d 1152, 1155, 185 U.S.P.Q. 644, 647 (C.C.P.A. 1975).

[In first full text paragraph, add after sentence ending in footnote 134:]

Whether two arts are or are not analogous is an issue on which there may not be universal agreement. It has been held that the toy building block art is not analogous to erecting roller conveyors.[134.1]

[134.1] Ex parte Vona Stein, 180 U.S.P.Q. 333 (P.O.Bd.App. 1973).

[Also in first full text paragraph, add after sentence ending with footnote 137:]

The mere fact that the disclosures can be combined does not make the combination obvious unless the art also contains something to suggest the desirability of the combination.[137.1]

[137.1] *In re* Imperator, 486 F.2d 585, 587, 179 U.S.P.Q. 730, 732 (D.C.C. 1967).

[Also in first full text paragraph, add after sentence ending with footnote 138:]

The Court of Customs & Patent Appeals has noted that a fertile imagination of the Examiner does not make a claimed invention obvious.[138.1]

[138.1] *In re* Way, 514 F.2d 1057, 1062, 185 U.S.P.Q. 580, 584 (C.C.P.A. 1975).

§ 6[3].   Under 35 U.S.C. 101

PAGE 241

[*Add text after sentence numbered "(3)":*]

A rejection alleging inoperativeness must be supported by more than an examiner's unsubstantiated doubt as to the invention's operability.[141.1]

[141.1] Ex parte Gastambide, 189 U.S.P.Q. 643 (P.O.Bd.App. 1974).

§ 6[4].   Under 35 U.S.C. 112

PAGE 241

[*In eighth text line of paragraph constituting this section, add after* "the claims.":]

The Examiner should specify on which paragraph of Section 112 he is relying.[141.2]

[141.2] *In re* Mayhew, 527 F.2d 1229, 1232, 188 U.S.P.Q. 356, 357-58 (C.C.P.A. 1976).

§ 6[4][a].   First paragraph

PAGE 241

[*Add text after last sentence in this section:*]

The Patent & Trademark Office has the burden of giving reasons, supported by the record as a whole, as to why the specification is not enabling.[143.1]

[143.1] *In re* Angstadt, 537 F.2d 498, 190 U.S.P.Q. 214 (C.C.P.A. 1976).

§ 6[4][b].   Second paragraph

PAGE 242

[*Add after first text paragraph on the page:*]

If the scope of the invention sought to be patented is unclear from the language of the claim, a Section 112, second paragraph rejection will properly lie.[147.1] The claims must make it clear what subject matter they encompass.[147.2]

[147.1] *In re* Wiggins, 488 F.2d 538, 541, 179 U.S.P.Q. 421, 423 (C.C.P.A. 1973).
[147.2] *In re* Conley, 490 F.2d 972, 975, 180 U.S.P.Q. 454, 456 (C.C.P.A. 1974).

[*Insert text immediately preceding paragraph denoted by* "[i] Duplicate Claims":]

At least the Board of Appeals has said that there need not always be a statutory basis for a rejection, in that judicially established doctrines are also proper basis for rejection.[149.1]

[149.1] Ex parte Haas, 188 U.S.P.Q. 374, 376-77 (P.O.Bd.App. 1975).

§ 6[5]. Under 35 U.S.C. 132

PAGE 243

[*Insert text between second and third paragraphs of this section:*]

Rejection under 35 U.S.C. 132 is tantamount to rejection under 35 U.S.C. 112, first paragraph, for lack of written description of the invention.[151.1]

[151.1] Wetmore v. Quick, 536 F.2d 937, 941, 190 U.S.P.Q. 223, 227 (C.C.P.A. 1976).

[*In third text line of fourth paragraph of the section, add after sentence ending in footnote* 152:]

An illustration of the cancellation of material from the specification constituting new matter would be the deletion of the proportions of the ingredients of a composition or the range in which a constituent would be effective for the purpose disclosed.

[*Insert text between fourth and fifth paragraphs of the section:*]

"New matter" has been judicially construed as having the same meaning in Section 251 as it does in the last sentence of Section

132.[153.1] Courts generally pay great deference to the opinion of the Examiner on the question of what constitutes new matter in amendment to a patent application.[153.2]

While the Patent Office has authority to restrict the specification so that it is not overbroad, it may not preclude an applicant from introducing amending language that would restrict an assertion to specific uses of a composition which uses are supported by proof contained in the record of the application. Accordingly, where the specification as originally filed merely recited "anti-tumour" activity, it was deemed not new matter for the applicant to qualify such wording with language specifying against which kinds of tumours the composition was demonstrated to be effective.[153.3]

[153.1] *In re* Hay, 534 F.2d 917, 919, 189 U.S.P.Q. 790, 791 (C.C.P.A. 1976).
[153.2] Milgo Electronics Corp. v. United Telecommunications, Inc., — F.Supp. —, —, 189 U.S.P.Q. 160, 169 (D.Kan. 1976).
[153.3] Rhone-Poulenc, S.A. v. Dann, 507 F.2d 261, 262, 184 U.S.P.Q. 196, 196 (4th Cir. 1974), *cert. denied* 422 U.S. 1009 (1975).

§ 7. Affidavit Practice

PAGE 243

[*Add text after first paragraph in the section:*]

It should be noted that in ex parte prosecution facts may be established by affidavit or declaration.[155.1] Such ex parte proofs, however, may not be relied upon in inter partes proceedings (as an interference).[155.2] The Court of Customs & Patent Appeals accepts statements in an appellant's disclosure as proof absent contrary evidence.[155.3] Mere arguments of counsel, however, cannot take the place of evidence.[155.4]

[155.1] *In re* Schneider, 481 F.2d 1350, 1355, 179 U.S.P.Q. 46, 50 (C.C.P.A. 1973).
[155.2] Natta v. Baxter, 179 U.S.P.Q. 692 (Bd.Pat.Int. 1973).
[155.3] *In re* Clinton, 188 U.S.P.Q. 365, 367 (C.C.P.A. 1976).
[155.4] *In re* Budnick, 537 F.2d 535, 537, 190 U.S.P.Q. 422, 424 (C.C.P.A. 1976).

§ 7.[1]. Rule 131

PAGE 244

[Insert text and illustration between first and second paragraphs of the section:]

A Rule 131 affidavit or declaration must establish that applicant's date of invention preceded the date of invention (that is, the date of actual reduction to practice) of the invention disclosed in the patent specification being applied by the examiner as a prior art reference; merely antedating the filing date of the patent may not be sufficient to obviate it as prior art.[156.1]

[156.1] *In re* Bass, 474 F.2d 1276, 177 U.S.P.Q. 178 (C.C.P.A. 1973).

To obviate as a reference, applicant's Rule 131 Affidavit must establish that applicant's invention date preceded patent's invention date.

Applicant's invention date	Patent's invention date	Patent's filing date	Applicant's filing date

[In sixth text line of second paragraph, add after "by an interference.":]

Accordingly, the law developed in Rule 131 cases is deemed of little bearing on the law relating to interference practice. A reference may be antedated in an ex parte proceeding by a lesser showing than would be required for winning a priority contest.[156.2]

[156.2] Wetmore v. Quick, 536 F.2d 937, 943, 190 U.S.P.Q. 223, 228 (C.C.P.A. 1976).

PAGE 245

[Insert text after paragraph ending in footnote **158***:]*

Declarations alleging that declarants were not the inventors of the invention being claimed, which invention was couched both in these declarations and in the claims in *generic* terms ("compounds having a hydroxyl group in a position ortho to an ozo linkage in a photoelectric imaging system") were deemed insufficient to overcome, as prior art, patent specifications naming declarants in the inventorship entities and disclosing *species* of the generic invention.[158.1]

[158.1] *In re* Carreira, 532 F.2d 356, 189 U.S.P.Q. 461 (C.C.P.A. 1976).

[In ninth text line of second paragraph following illustration, add footnote **159.1** *after* "must be shown."*:]*

[159.1] Satco, Inc. v. Transequip, Inc., 191 U.S.P.Q. 253, 254 (C.D.Cal. 1975).

[In same paragraph, delete all text after "Moreover, completion of applicant's invention, as he claims it, must be shown." *through end of the paragraph. Substitute:]*

Where, however, a claim is drawn to a generic invention, an affidavit or declaration showing completion of a species of that generic invention prior to the effective date of the reference will obviate that reference.[160] Furthermore, in ex parte practice, where the difference between what the reference relied upon by the examiner discloses and what the affidavit or declaration proffered pursuant to Rule 131 is obvious, the reference is deemed obviated.[160.1] In regard to inter partes practice, see *In re Barkowaki* and *In re Dardick*.[160.2] Speaking generally, the primary consideration in determining whether a prior art reference has been overcome is whether, in addition to showing what the reference shows, the affidavit or declaration also establishes possession of either the *whole* invention claimed or something falling *within* the claim, in the sense that the claims as a whole read on it.[160.3]

[160] *In re* Schaub, 537 F.2d 509, 190 U.S.P.Q. 324 (C.C.P.A. 1974); *In re* Stempel, 241 F.2d 755, 113 U.S.P.Q. 77 (C.C.P.A. 1957).

160.1 *In re* Spiller, 500 F.2d 1170, 182 U.S.P.Q. 614 (C.C.P.A. 1974); *In re* Stryker, 435 F.2d 1340, 168 U.S.P.Q. 372 (C.C.P.A. 1971).

160.2 505 F.2d 713, 184 U.S.P.Q. 29 (C.C.P.A. 1974); 496 F.2d 234, 181 U.S.P.Q. 834 (C.C.P.A. 1974).

160.3 *In re* Tanczyn, 347 F.2d 830, 833, 146 U.S.P.Q. 298, 300 (C.C.P.A. 1965).

§ 7[2][a]. Comparative tests or results

PAGE 246

*[Add text at end of the section, after footnote **163**:]*

The *specification,* however, need not allege superiority over the prior art with respect to a property or utility, if that property or utility (without an assertion of superiority) was originally disclosed, even generally, in the specification.[163.1]

163.1*In re* Slocombe, 510 F.2d 1398, 1403, 184 U.S.P.Q. 740, 743 (C.C.P.A. 1975); *In re* Lorenz, 333 F.2d 908, 912, 142 U.S.P.Q. 101, 104 (C.C.P.A. 1964).

§ 7[2][c]. Inoperability of references

PAGE 247

*[Add at end of the section, after footnote **166**:]*

It has been held that the inoperativeness of a machine does not ipso facto preclude its consideration as prior art.[166.1]

166.1 Louis A. Grant, Inc. v. Keibler Industries, Inc., 191 U.S.P.Q. 424, 426 (7th Cir. 1976); Stitter Products Co. v. Pettibone Mulliken Corp., 428 F.2d 639, 646-47, 166 U.S.P.Q. 100, 104-06 (7th Cir. 1970).

§ 7[2][e]. Sufficiency of disclosure

PAGE 247

*[Add at end of section, after footnote **168**:]*

An affidavit or declaration which merely recites conclusions, rather than facts, is insufficient to establish that a disclosure is adequate.[168.1]

168.1*In re* Brandstadter, 484 F.2d 1395, 1406, 179 U.S.P.Q. 286, 294 (C.C.P.A. 1973).

[Add new section:　§　7[2][f].]

[f] Nonobviousness

The Patent Office's failure to give weight to an affidavit from a prior art patentee to the effect that the improvement being claimed would not have been obvious to him was error.[168.2] A circuit court of appeals sustained summary judgment of invalidity notwithstanding that the record included the affidavit of a prior art inventor to the effect that the patentee's modification did not occur to him.[168.3]

[168.2]*In re* Meng, 492 F.2d 843, 181 U.S.P.Q. 94 (C.C.P.A. 1974). Compare, *In re* Rosaen, 477 F.2d 964, 177 U.S.P.Q. 577 (C.C.P.A. 1973); *In re* Ellis, 470 F.2d 1391, 170 U.S.P.Q. 309 (C.C.P.A. 1970).

[168.3]Research Corp. v. NASCO Industries, Inc., 501 F.2d 358, 182 U.S.P.Q. 449 (7th Cir. 1974).

§ 8.　Fraud on the Patent Office

PAGE 248

[Add text immediately preceding first full paragraph on the page:]

Such holding, however, was held, in a subsequent case brought by the patentee against another accused infringer, not to constitute an estoppel (under the circumstances in which the inequitable conduct had been brought to light in the first case) that would preclude the patentee from contending that its patent was not enforceable for fraud on the Patent Office.[170.1]

[170.1]Kearney & Trecker Corp. v. Cincinnati Milacron, Inc., 184 U.S.P.Q. 132 (S.D. Ohio 1974).

[Insert text after last full paragraph on the page:]

A charge of fraud, however, is not a mere trial tactic to be utilized when other defenses fail.[175.1]

[175.1]Paper Converting Machine Co. v. F.M.C. Corp., 179 U.S.P.Q. 78, 79 (D.Del. 1973).

[In last line of text on the page, add footnote 175.2 after "action for deceit,":]

[175.2]American Optical Corp. v. United States, 179 U.S.P.Q. 682, 684 (Ct.Cl. 1973).

PAGE 249

[Add to text after sentence numbered "(7)":]

However, some courts draw a distinction between fraud and inequitable conduct. A patent procured by fraud is invalid, whereas a patent tainted merely with inequitable conduct is unenforceable. A misrepresentation or concealment would suffice to constitute inequitable conduct, whereas all the elements necessary to establish a cause of action for common-law deceit would have to be present to establish fraud.[175.3]

Where infringement of more than one patent is charged, some courts have held all such patents unenforceable even though there was no evidence that all were fraudulently procured.[175.4] Other courts have held that it is only the patents actually touched by the fraud that are adversely affected.[175.5]

In order for a fraud defense to succeed at least two things must be established: (1) an element of willful, wrongful conduct or wrongful intent before the Patent Office; and (2) depending on the court, the wrongful conduct or intent must have either attempted to impair, or actually to have impaired, the Patent Office's ability to perform its statutory function, that is, to have been "material" or "relevant."[175.6] Unclean hands or fraud can be asserted only if there have been *deliberate misrepresentations* on the Patent Office.[175.7] An accused infringer that alleges that misrepresentations were made to the Patent Office must prove that the patent owner possessed knowledge of the facts and intentionally misrepresented or concealed them.[175.8] Mere negligent omissions or misstatements to the Patent Office do not provide sufficient basis for a conclusion of fraud or misrepresentation by the applicant.[175.9] Fraud standard is not one of strict liability for innocent or even negligent omissions or misstatements before the Patent Office.[175.10] Patents have been held invalid because of a failure to disclose to the Patent Office facts of which the applicant was aware and because applicant's arguments materially misrepresented contents of the prior art.[175.11]

However, misrepresentations made in an atmosphere of gross negligence as to their truth may be culpable.[175.12] Where an experiment was conducted in an incredibly sloppy manner, the patent was held unenforceable, though the court also found that the conduct of the patentee was not that of a party bent on deception. The patentee, however, failed an affirmative duty to investigate further the representations it made to the Patent Office when one of its people had reason to believe that representations made were erroneous.[175.13]

Concealment or omission to disclose may be as culpable as misrepresentation.[175.14] Where an applicant advises his patent attorney that specific prior art is perhaps the most similar to applicant's invention, such prior art should be cited specifically to the patent examiner.[175.15] Concealment of a prior sale by the patentee is so unconscionable an act as to provide a sufficient basis for award of attorney's fees under 35 U.S.C. 285.[175.16]

[175.3] Jack Winter, Inc. v. Koratron Co., 375 F. Supp. 1, 66, 181 U.S.P.Q. 353, 380-81 (N.D.Cal. 1974).

[175.4] East Chicago Machine Tool Corp. v. Stone Container Corp., 181 U.S.P.Q. 744 (N.D.Ill. 1974), modified 185 U.S.P.Q. 210 (N.D.Ill. 1975).

[175.5] Schlegel Mfg. Co. v. King Aluminum Corp., 381 F. Supp. 649, 184 U.S.P.Q. 22 (S.D.Ohio 1974); Saxton Products, Inc. v. U.S. Telephone Co., 182 U.S.P.Q. 608 (S.D.N.Y. 1974).

[175.6] In re Multidistrict Litigation Involving Frost Patent, 185 U.S.P.Q. 729, 741 (D.Del. 1975).

[175.7] Feed Service Corp. v. Kent Feeds, Inc., 528 F.2d 756, 762-63, 188 U.S.P.Q. 616, 621 (7th Cir. 1976).

[175.8] St. Regis Paper Co. v. Bemis Co., 403 F. Supp. 776, 785, 188 U.S.P.Q. 107, 115 (S.D.Ill. 1975).

[175.9] Parker v. Motorola, 524 F.2d 518, 534-35, 188 U.S.P.Q. 225, 238 (5th Cir. 1975).

[175.10] Pfizer, Inc. v. International Rectifier Corp., 538 F.2d 180, 186, 190 U.S.P.Q. 273, 278 (8th Cir. 1976); Schnadig Corp. v. Gaines Mfg. Co., 494 F.2d 383, 393, 181 U.S.P.Q. 417, 424 (6th Cir. 1974).

[175.11] Kahn v. Dynamics Corp. of America, 367 F. Supp. 63, 76, 180 U.S.P.Q. 247, 256 (S.D.N.Y. 1973).

[175.12] Norton v. Curtis, 433 F.2d 779, 797, 167 U.S.P.Q. 532, 546 (C.C.P.A. 1970).

[175.13] U.S. Movidyn Corp. v. Hercules, Inc., 388 F. Supp. 1146, 1154, 185 U.S.P.Q. 116, 122 (D.Minn. 1975).

[175.14] Layne-New York Co. v. Allied Asphalt Co., 363 F. Supp. 299, 307-08, 180 U.S.P.Q. 81, 87 (W.D.Pa. 1973).

[175.15] Borden, Inc. v. Occidental Petroleum Corp., 381 F. Supp. 1178, 1192, 182 U.S.P.Q. 474, 482 (S.D.Tex. 1974).

[175.16] Skil Corp. v. Lucerne Products, Inc., 503 F.2d 745, 183 U.S.P.Q. 396 (7th Cir. 1974).

[*In fifth text line of second full paragraph (page 249), insert new text after "duty to speak?":*]

It has been held that an omission or misrepresentation is material if it makes it impossible for the Patent Office fairly to assess a patent application against the prevailing statutory criteria.[176.1] Untrue statements and material misrepresentations weaken or destroy the presumption of validity.[176.2] Assignee who represented to the examiner that a certain element in the claims was novel, which element was known to be prior art by the assignee, constituted fraud on the Patent Office.[176.3]

[176.1] *In re* Multidistrict Litigation Involving the Frost Patent, 540 F.2d 601, 604, 191 U.S.P.Q. 241, 243 (3d Cir. 1976).

[176.2] Vollrath Co. v. Premium Plastics, Inc., 385 F. Supp. 843, 850, 183 U.S.P.Q. 335, 341 (N.D.Ill. 1974).

[176.3] Fruehauf Corp. v. International Terminal Co., 183 U.S.P.Q. 526 (D.N.J.), *aff'd* 508 F.2d 205, 184 U.S.P.Q. 266 (3d Cir. 1974).

[*In same paragraph (page 249), insert new text after sentence ending in footnote* **178**:]

Because the grant of a patent is infused with public interest, an applicant owes an uncompromising duty to report to the Patent Office all facts concerning possible fraud or inequitableness underlying application.[178.1] The duty of a patent attorney to the Patent Office is one of candor and leaves room for the exercise of good faith judgment even if that judgment is ultimately held to be faulty.[178.2] A potential exclusive licensee under an application has the same duty of candor to the Patent Office as does the applicant.[178.3] The duty to disclose to the Patent Office arises for matters that are relevant even though the applicant feels that they do not establish anticipation.[178.4] The citation to the Patent Office of too many publications that are clearly irrelevant and which can only clutter up the application may be just as obfuscating and misleading as excluding relevant prior art.[178.5] When an applicant slipped the important reference to the examiner in a list of twenty-two other references, this would reduce the weight of the presumption of validity.[178.6] An applicant who rushes the examiner to make a prior art reference of record must do more than merely submit the citation of such reference to the examiner.[178.7] However, at least one court has held that an attorney complies with his duty of candor by merely calling the references to the examiner's attention.[178.8]

An improper assertion of "criticality" in that the supposed criticality is either meaningless or spurious, constitutes fraud.[178.9] An applicant did not breach his duty of full and complete disclosure to the Patent Office by failing to inform the office that inherently defective prior art might work if process were performed according to applicant's teachings. There is no duty to disclose modifications which need to be made to a disclosure in order that it be a working invention.[178.10] Apparently, an applicant has no duty specifically to call to the attention of the Patent Office Board of Appeals a prior art reference that was cited but not relied upon by the examiner.[178.11]

178.1 Interlego A.G. v. F.A.O. Schwarz, Inc., 191 U.S.P.Q. 129, 136-37 (N.D.Ga. 1976).

178.2 Tokyo Shibaura Electric Co. v. Zenith Radio Corp., 404 F. Supp., 547, 569, 188 U.S.P.Q. 55, 71-72 (D.Del. 1975).

178.3 Maraine Products v. ICI America, Inc., 379 F. Supp., 261, 264, 181 U.S.P.Q. 498, 500 (N.D.Ill. 1974), *modified* 538 F.2d 134, —, 191 U.S.P.Q. 65 (7th Cir. 1976).

178.4 Turzillo v. P & Z Mergentime, 532 F.2d 1393, 1399, 189 U.S.P.Q. 783, 787-88 (D.C.C. 1976).

178.5 International Telephone & Telegraph Corp. v. Raychem Corp., 188 U.S.P.Q. 214, 222 (D.Mass. 1975), *aff'd* 538 F.2d 453, 191 U.S.P.Q. 1 (1st Cir. 1976).

178.6 Ropat Corp. v. West Bend Co., 382 F. Supp. 1030, 1035, 184 U.S.P.Q. 69, 73 (N.D.Ill. 1974).

178.7 Louis A. Grant, Inc. v. Keibler Industries, Inc., 377 F. Supp. 1069, 1082-83, 181 U.S.P.Q. 1, 11 (N.D.Ill. 1973).

178.8 Lundy Electronics, Inc. v. Optical Systems, Inc., 362 F. Supp. 130, 178 U.S.P.Q. 525, 534-35 (E.D.Va. 1973).

178.9 C.P.C. International, Inc. v. Standard Brands, Inc., 385 F. Supp. 1057, 1065-66, 184 U.S.P.Q. 332, 338-39 (D.Del. 1974); Bird Provision Co. v. Owens Country Sausage, Inc., 379 F. Supp. 744, 752-53, 184 U.S.P.Q. 174, 180 (N.D.Tex. 1974); Borden, Inc. v. Occidental Petroleum Corp., 381 F. Supp. 1178, 1192, 182 U.S.P.Q. 472, 482 (S.D.Tex. 1974).

178.10 Azoplate Corp. v. Silverlith, Inc., 367 F. Supp. 711, 726, 180 U.S.P.Q. 616, 626 (D.Del. 1973).

178.11 W.L. Gore & Associates, Inc. v. Carlisle Corp., 381 F. Supp. 680, 692, 183 U.S.P.Q. 459, 466 (D.Del. 1974).

[Add new text after last line on the page (still page 249):]

Fraud or unclean hands must be based on clear, unequivocal, and convincing evidence.[179.1] Fraud established in a Federal Trade Commission proceeding could be used to establish fraud in a judicial proceeding as the Federal Trade Commission proceeding did not require clear and convincing evidence.[179.2] Not every error occurring during patent prosecution amounts to fraud.[179.3] An "inadvertent" or "insignificant" error—as the use of an original application oath for a continuation-in-part application[179.4]—is not grounds for invalidating a patent. It was held not fraudulent to fail to disclose foreign counterparts in a continuation-in-part oath.[179.5]

That a foreign application was tainted with fraud would seem not *ipso facto* to vitiate its United States counterpart.[179.6]

The validity of a patent should not turn upon subsequent analysis of each step in the argument before the Patent Office, unless it appears that there was anticipation or obviousness.[179.7]

Absence of improper intent will preclude a finding of fraudulent procurement.[179.8] Good faith on the part of the patent owner obviates a contention that a patent should be declared invalid or unenforceable because of a failure to disclose information to the Patent Office.[179.9] A patent attorney or agent must have good faith belief in each assertion in an affidavit or declaration that he prepares for another's signature if that affidavit or declaration is to be submitted to the Patent Office.[179.10] Ex parte proceedings mandate a high standard of conduct and candor.[179.11]

[179.1] Feed Service Corp. v. Kent Feeds, Inc., 528 F.2d 756, 762-63, 188 U.S.P.Q. 616, 621 (7th Cir. 1976).

[179.2] State of North Carolina v. Chas. Pfizer & Co., 537 F.2d 67, 74, 189 U.S.P.Q. 262, 267 (4th Cir.), *cert. denied* 429 U.S. 870 (1976).

[179.3] Mooney v. Marlor, 190 U.S.P.Q. 207 (Comm.Pat. 1975).

[179.4] Cardinal of Adrian, Inc. v. Peerless Wood Products, Inc., 363 F. Supp. 1298, 1307, 179 U.S.P.Q. 527, 533 (E.D.Mich. 1973).

[179.5] Kelley Mfg. Co. v. Lilliston Corp., 180 U.S.P.Q. 364, 373 (E.D.N.C. 1973).

[179.6] Plantronics, Inc. v. Roanwell Corp., 185 U.S.P.Q. 505, 506 (S.D.N.Y. 1975); Amerace Corp. v. USM Corp., 185 U.S.P.Q. 525, 527 (N.D.Ill. 1975).

[179.7] Potter Instrument Co. v. Bucode, Inc., 184 U.S.P.Q. 662, 670 (E.D.N.Y. 1975).

[179.8] State of North Carolina v. Chas. Pfizer & Co., 384 F. Supp. 265, 282-83, 182 U.S.P.Q. 657, 668-69 (D.N.C. 1974), *aff'd* 537 F.2d 67, 189 U.S.P.Q. 262 (4th Cir.), *cert. denied* 429 U.S. 870 (1976).

[179.9] International Telephone & Telegraph Corp. v. Raychem Corp., 538 F.2d 453, 460-61, 191 U.S.P.Q. 1, 7-8 (1st Cir. 1976).

[179.10] Lund v. Bentley, 188 U.S.P.Q. 9, 13 (Bd.Pat.Int. 1974).

[179.11] *In re* Multidistrict Litigation Involving the Frost Patent, 540 F.2d 601, 611, 191 U.S.P.Q. 241, 249 (3d Cir. 1976).

§ 9. Correction of Defective Patents

§ 9[2]. Reissue Patents

PAGE 251

[*Insert new text between first and second paragraphs of the section:*]

At least one court has equated the "error without any deceptive intention" of the existing reissue statute with the "inadvertence, accident and mistake" criterion of the prior law.[184.1] The Court of Customs & Patent Appeals now takes the position that "error without any deceptive intention" is more liberal than the "inadvertence, accident and mistake" criterion of the prior law.[184.2] The Court of Customs & Patent Appeals has also taken the position that the patentability of reissue claims is to be determined by application of the law which exists during the prosecution of the reissue application rather than the law at the date of issuance of the original patent, where there has been a change since then.[184.3]

At least one court has equated "error without any deceptive intention" with an honest mistake.[184.4] One cannot add claims by reissue which are of the same scope as the claims in the original patent.[184.5]

[184.1] St. Regis Paper Co. v. Tee-Pak, Inc., 491 F.2d 1193, 1199-1200, 181 U.S.P.Q. 75, 79-81 (6th Cir. 1974).
[184.2] In re Wesseler, 367 F.2d 838, 151 U.S.P.Q. 339 (C.C.P.A. 1966), overruling In re Byers, 230 F.2d 451, 109 U.S.P.Q. 53 (C.C.P.A. 1956).
[184.3] In re Wadlinger, 496 F.2d 1200, 1208, 181 U.S.P.Q. 826, 832 (C.C.P.A. 1974).
[184.4] U.S. Industries, Inc. v. Norton Co., 184 U.S.P.Q. 187, 189 (N.D.N.Y. 1974).
[184.5] In re Wittry, 489 F.2d 1299, 180 U.S.P.Q. 320 (C.C.P.A. 1974).

[In second text paragraph, add after sentence ending in footnote 185:]

The Patent & Trademark Office may question the sufficiency of disclosure in a reissue application even where that disclosure was accepted in the corresponding original application.[185.1]

[185.1] In re Doyle, 482 F.2d 1385, 179 U.S.P.Q. 227 (C.C.P.A. 1973), cert. denied 416 U.S. 935 (1974).

[Add text at end of second paragraph, after footnote 187:]

An application for a narrowed reissue may not be denied on the grounds of delay or lack of diligence in filing the reissue application, absent equitable considerations.[187.1]

[187.1] Ex parte Lafferty, 190 U.S.P.Q. 202 (P.O.Bd.App. 1975).

[Add text after last line on the page (page 251):]

However, the claim of a reissue patent was invalidated where its scope was essentially that of claims in the original patent that had been canceled in order to secure allowance.[193.1] A reissue patent is *not* available where the original patent has been declared invalid.

The reissue statute may cure the sick, but it cannot raise the dead.[193.2] A rationale for refusing to reissue a patent declared to be invalid may be based upon the Supreme Court's ruling in *Blonder-Tongue Laboratories, Inc. v. University of Illinois Foundation*[193.3] that district courts shall not consider in infringement action any claim that has previously been held invalid.[193.4]

[193.1] Potter Instrument Co. v. ODEC Computer Systems, Inc., 370 F. Supp. 198, 181 U.S.P.Q. 572 (D.R.I. 1974).

[193.2] *In re* Hay, 534 F.2d 917, 189 U.S.P.Q. 790 (C.C.P.A. 1976).

[193.3] 402 U.S. 313, 169 U.S.P.Q. 513 (1971).

[193.4] Ex parte Varga, 189 U.S.P.Q. 204 (P.O.Bd.App. 1973).

Notes

PAGE 253

[*Add to footnote* **29**:]

M.P.E.P. 706.03(W).

PAGE 254

[*Add to footnote* **71**:]

Grall v. Dann, 188 U.S.P.Q. 95 (D.D.C. 1975).

[*Add to footnote* **76**:]

In re Varga, 511 F.2d 1175, 185 U.S.P.Q. 47 (C.C.P.A. 1975).

PAGE 255

[*Add to footnote* **123**:]

In re Outtrup, 531 F.2d 1055, 189 U.S.P.Q. 345 (C.C.P.A. 1976); *In re* Coker, 463 F.2d 1344, 175 U.S.P.Q. 26 (C.C.P.A. 1972); *In re* Sheppard, 339 F.2d 238, 144 U.S.P.Q. 42 (C.C.P.A. 1964).

[*Add to footnote* **124**:]

In re Langer, 503 F.2d 1380, 1391, 183 U.S.P.Q. 288, 296-97 (C.C.P.A. 1974).

[*Add to footnote* **129**:]

In re Neil, 481 F.2d 1346, 1347, 179 U.S.P.Q. 56, 57 (C.C.P.A. 1973); Ex parte Varga, 189 U.S.P.Q. 204 (P.O.Bd.App. 1973).

PAGE 256

[*Add to footnote* **133**:]

Ex parte Thompson, 184 U.S.P.Q. 558, 559 (P.O.Bd.App. 1974).

[*Add to footnote* **137**:]

In re Regel, 526 F.2d 1399, 1403, 188 U.S.P.Q. 136 (C.C.P.A. 1975).

[*Add to footnote* **143**:]

In re Gaffee, 526 F.2d 1393, 1397-98, 188 U.S.P.Q. 131, 135 (C.C.P.A. 1975).

PAGE 257

[*Add to footnote* **175**:]

Zenith Laboratories, Inc. v. Carter-Wallace, Inc., 530 F.2d 508, 514, 189 U.S.P.Q. 387, 392 (3d Cir. 1976).

[*Add to footnote* **177**:]

Farmer Brothers Co. v. Coca-Cola Co., 184 U.S.P.Q. 587, 589 (C.D.Cal. 1974); Mayview Corp. v. Rodstein, 385 F. Supp. 1122, 1126, 184 U.S.P.Q. 466, 468-69 (C.D.Cal. 1974); Borden, Inc. v. Occidental Petroleum Corp., 381 F. Supp. 1178, 1192, 182 U.S.P.Q. 472, 482 (S.D.Tex. 1974); Borden, Inc. v. Kerr-McGee Chemical Co., 182 U.S.P.Q. 307, 311-12 (E.D.Mich. 1974).

[*Add to footnote* **187**:]

Cohen v. United States, 179 U.S.P.Q. 859, 861 (Ct.Cl. 1973).

Chapter 14

LICENSING AND ASSIGNMENT:
THE SHARING AND TRANSFER OF PATENT RIGHTS

PAGE 263

[Add text after quotation from Section 261:]

The written instrument that transfers an interest in a patent must be unambiguous and show a clear and unmistakable intent to part with that interest. Although no particular formula of words is essential, it must be apparent from the instrument that there was a clear intent of the assignor to part with his legal interest.[a1]

[a1] Potlatch Corp. v. Innovations, Inc., 189 U.S.P.Q. 436, 437-38 (N.D.Ill. 1975).

[In eighth text line of third full paragraph, add after "to another.":]

The validity of an assignment of patent rights, as between the parties, is not affected by the failure to record the assignment.[2.1]

[2.1] Eickmeyer v. Commissioner of Internal Revenue, 190 U.S.P.Q. 31, 35 (U.S.T.C. 1976).

[Add immediately preceding last text paragraph on the page:]

Failure to execute an assignment after entering into a contract to assign a patent is analogous to recording an assignment in the Patent & Trademark Office. In either instance legal title may pass. A contract provision that patent assignment would be placed in escrow to be delivered for recordation in the Patent & Trademark Office when the buyer pays in full the unpaid balance, and that until that time the buyer shall have no right to mortgage the patent, is a mere formality designed to guarantee payment and facilitate recordation; it is not a reservation of legal title where the contract to assign the patent states that the seller "hereby sells [the patent] to the buyer."[2.2]

[2.2] Sims v. Mack Trucks, Inc., 407 F. Supp. 742, 744, 191 U.S.P.Q. 218, 219 (E.D.Pa. 1976).

PAGE 264

[Add immediately after first line of text on the page:]

The assignment of a patent does not carry along with it the assignment of the lawyer or law firm that formerly represented the assignor.[2.3]

[2.3] *In re* Yarn Processing Patent Validity Litigation, 530 F.2d 83, 90, 190 U.S.P.Q. 523, 527 (5th Cir. 1976).

[*In first full text paragraph, add after sentence ending in footnote* 3:]

Cases that have required the patentee to be a party to a suit for patent infringement are situations where the assignor reserved certain rights over the patent.[3.1]

[3.1] TWM Manufacturing Co. v. Dura Corp., — F. Supp. —, 189 U.S.P.Q. 518, 526 (E.D.Mich. 1975).

[*In 11th line of same text paragraph, add after* "his own invention!":]

An absolute exclusive license prevents the licensor from granting any license other than the immediate one. A license accompanied by a covenant that the licensor will not grant any other licenses without the consent of the immediate licensee permits licensor to grant other licenses under the specified conditions.[4.1]

[4.1] Moraine Products v. ICI America, Inc., 538 F.2d 134, 141, 191 U.S.P.Q. 65, 71 (7th Cir. 1976).

[*Insert text between first and second full paragraphs:*]

In fact, it has been held that an exclusive licensee can sue a licensor for patent infringement, and the fact that the status of the exclusivity of the license is in dispute does not affect the court's jurisdiction.[5.1] Moreover, retention of royalty rights does not in and of itself negate assignment.[5.2] One who "assigns" a patent but retains the right to royalties and performance of other services, in default of which patent immediately reverts back to the assignor, is indistinguishable from one who grants an exclusive and revocable patent license.[5.3]

[5.1] Sumner v. The Sumner Sales Agency, Inc., 188 U.S.P.Q. 396, 400 (N.D.Tex. 1975).
[5.2] TWM Manufacturing Co. v. Dura Corp., 189 U.S.P.Q. 518, 526 (E.D.Mich. 1975).
[5.3] Hanes Corp. v. Millard, 531 F.2d 585, 593, 189 U.S.P.Q. 331, 336-37 (D.D.C. 1976).

[*In second text line of second full paragraph, add footnote* 5.4 *after* "licensees."]

⁵·⁴ Moraine Products v. ICI America, Inc., 538 F.2d 134, 143, 191 U.S.P.Q. 65, 73 (7th Cir. 1976), citing PATENT LAW FUNDAMENTALS.

[After last text line on the page (page 264), add:]

The name given an instrument is not determinative. The true test as to its nature is its "legal effect."⁶·¹

⁶·¹ Von Brimer v. Whirlpool Corp., 536 F.2d 838, 844, 190 U.S.P.Q. 528, 532 (9th Cir. 1976).

PAGE 265

[Add text immediately preceding first full paragraph on the page:]

The subject matter of what is being licensed is whatever "reads on" or is "covered by" the claims of the patent.⁶·²

⁶·² Richen-Gemco, Inc. v. Heltra, Inc., 540 F.2d 1235, 1239, 191 U.S.P.Q. 663, 665 (4th Cir. 1976).

§ 1. Provisions Relating to the Extent of Patent Rights Conveyed or Licensed

§ 1[4]. Geographic

PAGE 267

[Add text after the paragraph constituting this section:]

The permissiveness of Section 261 in regard to the division of domestic patent rights among different parts of the United States has been extended to world markets. Thus, a provision in a patent license granting foreign rights but forbidding the foreign licensees from exporting to the United States was held not to constitute an illegal division of world markets violating the antitrust laws, Section 261 being cited as authority for this holding.¹⁵·¹

¹⁵·¹ Dunlop Co., Ltd. v. Kelsey-Hayes Co., 484 F.2d 407, 179 U.S.P.Q. 129 (6th Cir. 1973).

§ 2. Ancillary Provisions

§ 2[1][a]. Money payments

PAGE 268

[Insert text between first and second paragraphs:]

Absent overriding unlawful conduct, it is not a patent misuse to offer a license only at what an accused infringer considers an exorbitant price. Royalty demand so high as to preclude acceptance of license is not appreciably different from a refusal to license upon any terms. The right to refuse to license is the essence of patent holder's right under the patent law.[18.1]

[18.1] W.L. Gore & Associates, Inc. v. Carlisle Corp., 529 F.2d 614, 623, 189 U.S.P.Q. 129, 136 (3d Cir. 1976).

§ 2[1][b]. Exchange of patent rights

PAGE 270

[Insert between first and second full text paragraphs:]

However, merely that a package license does not provide for the lowering or elimination of royalties as licensed patents expire does not in and of itself warrant a finding of patent misuse unless the patentee coerced the licensee to pay royalties on a group of patents.[27.1]

It has been held *not* a patent misuse for a patent holder to refuse to continue to do business with a willful infringer, thereby possibly contributing financially to the ability of the latter to defend against and possibly defeat his infringement suit. A patent holder has the right in common with all others to do business with whom he pleases.[27.2]

[27.1] Mobil Oil Corp. v. W.R. Grace & Co., 367 F. Supp. 207, 257, 180 U.S.P.Q. 418, 452-53 (D.Conn. 1973).
[27.2] W.L. Gore & Associates, Inc. v. Carlisle Corp., 529 F.2d 614, 624, 189 U.S.P.Q. 129, 137 (3d Cir. 1976).

[Add text immediately preceding last paragraph on the page:]

There is nothing intrinsically unlawful in licenses which grant access to more than one patent. The key question is whether the licensee was coerced to accept a license under more patents than it desired.[28.1]

[28.1] Mobil Oil Corp. v. W.R. Grace & Co., 367 F. Supp. 207, 257, 180 U.S.P.Q. 418, 452 (D.Conn. 1973).

§ 2[1][c]. Cessation of royalty payments

PAGE 272

[*In sixth text line on the page, add after* "patented invention.".]

"Eviction" from a license occurs when the patent is adjudged invalid so that there is a complete failure of consideration.[33.1]

[33.1] Zenith Laboratories, Inc. v. Carter-Wallace, Inc., 530 F.2d 508, 513, 189 U.S.P.Q. 387, 391 (3d Cir.), *cert. denied* 429 U.S. 828 (1976).

§ 2[4]. Most-Favored Licensee

PAGE 273

[*Add text at end of the section:*]

An interesting question regarding the effect of a most-favored licensee clause is whether forgiveness of licensor's past infringement in exchange for the payment of royalties for prospective use entitles the most-favored licensee to a return of royalties paid during the period of the other party's infringement. It was held that the duty to stop infringement by others did not imply under a most-favored licensee clause a duty to recover a sum certain for past infringement in order for the licensor not to forfeit the right to royalty payments during the period of infringement.[38.1] However, in another case, it was said that the full consideration paid by each licensee is material in determining whether a most-favored licensee is entitled to more favorable rates.[38.2]

[38.1] Searle Analytic, Inc. v. Ohio-Nuclear, Inc., 187 U.S.P.Q. 360, 398 F. Supp. 229 (N.D.Ill. 1975).
[38.2] Shatterproof Glass Corp. v. Libbey-Owens-Ford Co., 482 F.2d 317, 324, 179 U.S.P.Q. 3, 8 (6th Cir. 1976), *cert. denied.*

§ 2[5]. Miscellaneous Provisions

PAGE 274

[*Add after second text line on the page:*]

There is a distinction between a mere choice of law provision and a voluntary submission to personal jurisdiction. Accordingly, the presence of a choice of law provision in a patent license agreement stipulating that the law of New York was to control any dispute arising under the agreement did not amount to the submission by the parties thereto to personal jurisdiction in New York.[38.3]

Courts do not look with favor upon the arbitration of patent infringement disputes as they involve questions of public interest. Accordingly, it has been held that such disputes are inappropriate for determination by arbitration proceedings, participation therein having been enjoined.[38.4]

A clause in a licensing agreement prohibiting the licensee from contesting validity was held unenforceable, but not in and of itself a patent misuse.[38.5]

[38.3] McShan v. Omega Louis Brandt et Frère, S.A., 536 F.2d 516, 518, 191 U.S.P.Q. 8, 10 (2d Cir. 1976).

[38.4] N.A. Maatschappy Voor Industriele Waarden v. A.O. Smith Corp., 532 F.2d 874, 190 U.S.P.Q. 385 (2d Cir. 1976); Hanes Corp. v. Millard, 531 F.2d 585, 189 U.S.P.Q. 331 (D.C.C. 1976); Duplan Corp. v. Deering Milliken, Inc., 540 F.2d 1215, 191 U.S.P.Q. 417 (4th Cir. 1976); Babcock & Wilcox Co. v. Public Service Co. of Indiana, Inc., — F. Supp. —, 193 U.S.P.Q. 161, — (S.D.Ind. 1976); Diematic Mfg. Corp. v. Packaging Industries, Inc., 381 F. Supp. 1057, 184 U.S.P.Q. 410 (S.D.N.Y. 1974).

[38.5] Congoleum Industries, Inc. v. Armstrong Coke Co., 366 F. Supp. 220, 180 U.S.P.Q. 264, 270 (E.D.Pa. 1973).

§ 4.   Antitrust Analysis and Critique

§ 4[1].   Sherman Act, Section 1

PAGE 276

[*In fifth text line of first paragraph of the section add footnote* **45.1** *after* "tion.":]

[45.1] Moraine Products v. ICI America, Inc., 538 F.2d 134, 146, 191 U.S.P.Q. 65, 75 (7th Cir. 1976).

PAGE 277

[*Add new text at end of section:*]

Also culpable under the Sherman Act, Section 1, is the use of patent licenses as a cover for part of a larger conspiracy or combination in restraint of trade.[48.1] The refusal of a patent owner to license when that refusal is pursuant to a conspiracy or combination, may be objectionable under the antitrust laws, based on anticompetitive possibilities.[48.2] Whether a particular policy or course of conduct in granting or refusing to grant a patent license is violative of the antitrust laws is to be determined by the application of "Rule of Reason" analysis and not by a per se approach.[48.3]

The settlement of patent litigation, in and of itself, does not violate the antitrust laws, where there are legitimate conflicting patent claims or threatened interferences. Settlement by agreement, rather than by litigation, is not precluded by the Sherman Act. It is only where settlement agreements are entered into in bad faith and are utilized as part of a scheme to restrain or monopolize trade that antitrust violations may occur.[48.4]

[48.1] See, for example, United States v. Line Material Co., 333 U.S. 287, 76 U.S.P.Q. 399 (1948); United States v. U.S. Gypsum Co., 333 U.S. 364, 76 U.S.P.Q. 430 (1948).

[48.2] Moraine Products v. ICI America, Inc., 538 F.2d 134, 141, 191 U.S.P.Q. 65, 71-72 (7th Cir. 1976).

[48.3] Moraine Products v. ICI America, Inc., 538 F.2d 134, 145, 191 U.S.P.Q. 65, 74 (7th Cir. 1976).

[48.4] The Duplan Corp. v. Deering Milliken, Inc., 540 F.2d 1215, 1220-22, 191 U.S.P.Q. 417, 421-22 (4th Cir. 1976).

§ 4[2]. Clayton Act, Section 2

PAGE 277

[In 18th text line of paragraph constituting this section, add after "patent misuse.":]

Moreover, courts will not aid a patent holder who abused a patent to recover any emoluments accruing during the period of his misuse. The patent misuse doctrine is an extension of the equitable doctrine that denies judicial relief to one coming into court with "unclean hands." Courts will not protect a patent monopoly that is being used to restrain competition, contrary to the policy of the antitrust laws, even if an antitrust violation has not been proved.[49.1]

[49.1] W.L. Gore & Associates, Inc. v. Carlisle Corp., 529 F.2d 614, 189 U.S.P.Q. 129 (3d Cir. 1976).

§ 5. Tax Treatment of Patents

§ 5[1]. Transfer

PAGE 279

[*In fourth text line of last paragraph on the page, delete* "a six month holding period." *and the next sentence. Substitute:*]

the holding period. Section 1403 of the Tax Reform Act of 1976 amends Section 1222 of the Internal Revenue Code by increasing the duration of the holding period needed to qualify for long-term capital gains treatment from six months to eight months in 1976, and to ten months in 1977, and to one year in 1978 and thereafter. P.L. 94-455, 90 Stat. 1520. An asset which has been held for more than the requisite holding period is to be treated as a long-term or capital asset in the hands of that holder.

PAGE 280

[*Add to text after sentence ending in footnote* **67:**]

The question of whether "all substantial rights" to a patent have been transferred is generally resolved by examining the substantiality of rights, if any, that the transferor has retained. The transfer of the right to make, use, and vend is deemed to constitute an assignment of "all substantial rights" in the patent; transfer of anything less is a mere license. Retention of the absolute right to prohibit sublicensing may or may not constitute a retention of substantial rights, depending on circumstances.[67.1] The last of a series of limited licenses, that is, the one that finally exhausts "all substantial rights" owned by the patentee, is entitled to capital gains treatment even if the prior licenses were not.[67.2]

An "undivided interest" to be entitled to capital gains treatment need not be of a specific amount. The size or extent of the undivided interest transferred is not relevant in determining whether the transfer of patent rights qualifies for Section 1235 capital gains treatment.[67.3]

[67.1] Eickmeyer v. Commissioner of Internal Revenue, 190 U.S.P.Q. 31 (U.S.T.C. 1976).
[67.2] Blake v. Commissioner of Internal Revenue, 192 U.S.P.Q. 45 (U.S.T.C. 1976).
[67.3] Eickmeyer v. Commissioner of Internal Revenue, 190 U.S.P.Q. 31 (U.S.T.C. 1976).

PAGE 281

[*Add new section:* § **5[4].**]

[4] Employee Achievement Awards

Amount paid to an employee pursuant to an invention achievement award plan was ordinary income paid by the employer.[74]

[74] Beausoleil v. Commissioner of Internal Revenue, 190 U.S.P.Q. 348 (U.S.T.C. 1976).

Notes

PAGE 282

[*Add to footnote* 1:]

Western Electric Co. v. Milgo Electronic Corp., 190 U.S.P.Q. 546, 549 (S.D.Fla. 1976).

PAGE 283

[*Add to footnote* 54:]

Zenith Laboratories, Inc. v. Carter-Wallace, Inc., 530 F.2d 508, 514, 189 U.S.P.Q. 387, 392 (3d Cir. 1976).

PAGE 284

[*Add to footnote* 67:]

Klein v. Commissioner of Internal Revenue, 507 F.2d 617, 184 U.S.P.Q. 617 (7th Cir. 1974); Mros v. Commissioner of Internal Revenue, 493 F.2d 813, 181 U.S.P.Q. 487 (9th Cir. 1974); Fawick v. Commissioner of Internal Revenue, 436 F.2d 655, 162 U.S.P.Q. 185 (6th Cir. 1971).

Chapter 15

LITIGATION: THE ENFORCEMENT OF PATENT RIGHTS

PAGE 286

[*In the fifth text line of third full paragraph on the page, add after* "process of procuring a patent.":]

However, at least one court has deemed a Patent Office interference proceeding as "litigation" coming within the penumbra of the work-product doctrine.[2.1]

[2.1] Talley Industries v. United States, 188 U.S.P.Q. 368, 370 (Ct.Cl. 1975).

§ 2. Patent Infringement

PAGE 288

[*In fourth text line of first paragraph of this section, add immediately preceding* "If a patent is analogized to real property,":]

Consequently, the terminology "patent infringement" is misleading since it is the *claims* of a patent which are infringed.[13.1]

[13.1] CTS Corp. v. Piher International Corp., 527 F.2d 95, 100, 188 U.S.P.Q. 419, 423 (7th Cir. 1975).

PAGE 289

[*Add text after paragraph ending in* "(2) contributory infringement.":]

The 1952 Patent Act codified three torts of a patent infringement. Contributing to direct infringement and specifically intending to induce direct infringement are separate torts of indirect infringement that overlap in many instances, but specific intent to cause direct infringement that is required to establish inducement is not a necessary element of contributory infringement. The sale of a nonstaple article having no known noninfringing use is not a necessary element of the tort of inducement. Section 271 is the first congressional effort to codify the common law doctrines of patent infringement. The facts addressed in *Mercoid v. Mid-Continent Investment Co.*[14.1] would not mandate a different conclusion under Section 271.[14.2]

[14.1] 320 U.S. 661, 60 U.S.P.Q. 21.
[14.2] Rohm & Haas Co. v. Dawson Chemical Co., 191 U.S.P.Q. 691, 699 (S.D.Tex. 1976).

[Add to text after paragraph ending in "any of its claims."*:]*

United States patent laws protect only domestic markets. Thus the making, using or selling of a patented invention outside the United States is not proscribed unless it induces or contributes to a domestic infringement.[14.3]

[14.3] Engineering Sports v. Brunswick Corp., 179 U.S.P.Q. 486, 488 (D.Utah 1973).

PAGE 291

[Add immediately preceding first full text paragraph on the page:]

Infringement by inducement occurred where labels on cans of staple resin included instructions on how to use the contents in a manner that would infringe.[15.1] Where a manufacturer carried out all but the last steps of the claimed process, the manufacturer's customer carrying out the last step, the court held the manufacturer liable as a direct infringer by in effect treating the manufacturer's customers as the agents of the manufacturer.[15.2]

[15.1] Rex Chainbelt, Inc. v. Harco Products, Inc., 181 U.S.P.Q. 432 (C.D.Cal. 1973).
[15.2] Mobil Oil Corp. v. W.R. Grace & Co., 367 F. Supp. 207, 253, 180 U.S.P.Q. 418, 450 (D.Conn. 1973).

[In 12th text line of last paragraph on the page, add footnote **18.1** *after the words* "constitute infringement."*:]*

[18.1] High Voltage Engineering Corp. v. Potentials, Inc., 398 F. Supp. 18, 19, 188 U.S.P.Q. 535, 536 (W.D.Tex. 1974).

[Add after last text line on the page:]

Whether a patented device is reconstructed or not depends on each case's peculiar facts. An overhaul operation that resulted in breathing new life into a spent patented combination was impermissible reconstruction. A patented combination of seventeen basic unpatented elements ceased to exist when the device was disassembled into its four basic components.[19.1]

The right of the owner of a patented combination to repair may be couched in terms of an implied license. A similar approach has been taken in regard to the purchase from the patentee of a composition with instructions supplied by the patentee on how to use the composition. In such case, the purchaser was deemed to have an implied license to carry out the instructions even though they read on the patentee's method claims.[19.2]

[19.1] General Electric Co. v. United States, 191 U.S.P.Q. 594, 621 (Ct.Cl. 1976).
[19.2] Rohm & Haas Co. v. Dawson Chemical Co., 191 U.S.P.Q. 691, 696 (S.D.Tex. 1976).

PAGE 292

[*Insert between first and second text paragraphs on the page:*]

Motive or intent with which alleged act of infringement is committed is immaterial. A person may infringe a patent without actual knowledge of its existence.[20.1] Thus, infringement because of malfunction is still infringement.[20.2]

No infringement, neither direct nor contributory, can occur until the patent is issued. Consequently, damages cannot begin to accrue until the patent is issued.[20.3]

[20.1] Milgo Electronics Corp. v. United Telecommunications, 189 U.S.P.Q. 160, 169 (D.Kan. 1976).
[20.2] Hughes Tool Co. v. G.W. Murphy Industries, Inc., 491 F.2d 923, 927-28, 180 U.S.P.Q. 353, 356 (5th Cir. 1973).
[20.3] St. Regis Paper Co. v. Benis Co., 403 F. Supp. 776, 781, 188 U.S.P.Q. 107, 112 (S.D.Ill. 1975).

[*At end of second text paragraph, add footnote* **20.4** *after the words* "to the world.":]

[20.4] M & T Chemicals, Inc. v. International Business Machines Corp., 403 F. Supp. 1145, 1148, 188 U.S.P.Q. 568, 570 (S.D.N.Y. 1975).

[*In seventh text line of fourth paragraph, add footnote* **21.1** *after the words* "to be immaterial." *and add new text:*]

to be immaterial.[21.1] A corporate officer is generally not personally liable for infringement when he acts solely within his duties as an officer and director.[21.2]

21.1 Milgo Electronics Corp. v. United Telecommunications, 189 U.S.P.Q. 160, 169 (D.Kan. 1976).

21.2 U.S. Philips Corp. v. National Micronetics, Inc., 410 F. Supp. 449, 468, 188 U.S.P.Q. 662, 678 (S.D.N.Y. 1976).

[*Insert text immediately preceding last full paragraph on the page (page 292):*]

The manufacture and experimental use of a machine has been held not to constitute an infringement until the machine is put to a commercially valuable use.[22.1] However, an experimental use by the Government has been deemed an infringement for which the patentee is entitled to just compensation.[22.2] The doctrine of de minimus non curat lex has been invoked to deny compensation for a single act of infringement during the early planning stages of a space mission.[22.3]

Infringement is not avoided by the addition of other steps or embellishments to a patented process or by imperfect practice of patented invention, such as weak rather than strong embossing.[22.4] Imperfect infringement is nonetheless infringement.[22.5] Impairment of function and lessening of result, in degree only, does not avoid infringement.[22.6] Infringement because of malfunction is still infringement.[22.7]

Pictures appearing in a catalogue are not acts of infringement.[22.8]

Using a single means to perform same function in same manner as two separate means does not avoid infringement.[22.9]

An accused infringer that sells but does not manufacture the accused product cannot infringe patent's *process* claims.[22.10]

22.1 Levin v. Ripple Truist Mills, Inc., 416 F. Supp. 876, 881, 191 U.S.P.Q. 38, 42 (E.D.Pa. 1976).

22.2 Douglas v. United States, 181 U.S.P.Q. 170 (Ct.Cl. 1974).

22.3 Finney v. United States, 188 U.S.P.Q. 33 (Ct.Cl. 1975).

22.4 Armstrong Cork Co. v. Congoleum Industries, Inc., 399 F. Supp. 1141, 1152, 188 U.S.P.Q. 679, 688 (E.D.Pa. 1975).

22.5 Lawrence Rigging, Inc. v. Airtek Corp., 182 U.S.P.Q. 375, 378 (D.Mass. 1974).

22.6 Milgo Electronics Corp. v. United Telecommunications, 189 U.S.P.Q. 160, 169 (D.Kan. 1976).

22.7 Hughes Tool Co. v. G.W. Murphy Industries, Inc., 491 F.2d 923, 926-27, 180 U.S.P.Q. 353, 355-56 (5th Cir. 1973).

[22.8] Molinaro v. Sears, Roebuck & Co., — F. Supp. —, —, 183 U.S.P.Q. 677, 679 (N.D.Pa. 1974).
[22.9] Lockheed Aircraft Corp. v. United States, — F.2d —, —, 190 U.S.P.Q. 134, 147.(Ct.Cl. 1976).
[22.10] Grain Products, Inc. v. Lincoln Grain, Inc., 191 U.S.P.Q. 177, 179 (S.D.Ill. 1976).

PAGE 293

[Add text after paragraph ending in footnote 26:]

Savings realized by the infringer as a result of his infringement are sometimes used as the measure of compensation. Where the infringing use is authorized by or consented to by the United States and an established royalty rate is shown to exist, that rate will usually be adopted as the best measure of reasonable and entire compensation.[26.1] Concept of a reasonable royalty represents the minimum of damages provided by 35 U.S.C. 284, which allows trebling of damages. Factor by which damages are multiplied is within the sound discretion of the court. United States district court may set damages above the license royalty rate, where it also determines that royalty rate was artificially depressed by ongoing infringement. A district court in calculating damages may focus on patent owner's losses rather than profits illegally made by infringer. But however a district court fixes damages, it must explain how the particular level chosen was related to the evidence proffered by the parties.[26.2]

[26.1] Tektronix, Inc. v. United States, 188 U.S.P.Q. 25, 29 (Ct.Cl. 1975).
[26.2] Trio Process Corp. v. L. Goldstein's Sons, Inc., 533 F.2d 126, 189 U.S.P.Q. 561 (3d Cir. 1976). See also, Spould v. Mohasco Industries, Inc., 534 F.2d 404, 190 U.S.P.Q. 1 (1st Cir. 1976).

PAGE 294

[In third text line on the page, add footnote 30.1 after "components.":]

[30.1] Hughes Tool Co. v. G.W. Murphy Industries, Inc., 491 F.2d 923, 928-29, 180 U.S.P.Q. 353, 357 (5th Cir. 1973).

[Add text immediately preceding first full paragraph on the page:]

Where the profits of an infringer attributable to infringement and noninfringement cannot be separated "the law places the loss on the wrongdoer."[31.1]

[31.1] American Sterilizer Co. v. Sybron Corp., 526 F.2d 542, 548-49, 188 U.S.P.Q. 97, 102 (3d Cir. 1975).

[In second text line of first full paragraph, add after sentence ending in footnote **32**:]

Double damages have been awarded a patent owner against an infringer that was aware of the existence of the patents from the time it started infringing.[32.1]

[32.1] St. Regis Paper Co. v. Winchester Corp., 410 F. Supp. 1304, 1309, 189 U.S.P.Q. 514, 518 (D.Mass. 1976).

[Insert text between first and second full paragraphs:]

Section 283 of the Patent Act permits a court to grant equitable relief as a remedy for patent infringement:

> The several courts having jurisdiction of cases under this title 35 U.S.C. may grant injunctions in accordance with the principles of equity to prevent the violation of any right secured by patent, on such terms as the court deems reasonable.

While it is only by means of injunctive relief that a patentee can realize "the right to exclude others" (35 U.S.C. 154), courts have declined to issue injunctions where: (1) an injunction would have meant that the infringer would have been out of business and the patentee would get no future royalties because he was not himself engaged in the exploitation of his invention.[32.2] And (2), where a license had been refused by the patentee "solely because of a personal feud between plaintiffs and defendants."[32.3]

[32.2] Foster v. American Machine & Foundry Co., 492 F.2d 1317, 182 U.S.P.Q. 1 (2d Cir. 1974).
[32.3] Allied Research Products, Inc. v. Heatbath Corp., 300 F.Supp. 656, 161 U.S.P.Q. 527 (N.D.Ill. 1969).

PAGE 295

[In second text line of first paragraph on the page, add after sentence ending in footnote **34**:]

The presumption of patent validity is weakened when the patent examiner did not consider all pertinent art.[34.1] Some courts go so far as to say that the statutory presumption of validity *does not apply* to prior art not cited by the Patent Office and that even one prior art reference not cited by the examiner overcomes the presumption of validity.[34.2]

[34.1] U.S. Philips Corp. v. National Micronetics, Inc., — F. Supp. —, —, 188 U.S.P.Q. 662, 671 (S.D.N.Y. 1976).

[34.2] Turzillo v. P & Z Mergentime, 532 F.2d 1393, 1399, 189 U.S.P.Q. 783, 787 (D.C.C. 1976).

[In same paragraph, add after footnote 35:]

Thus, the fact that the claims of a patent had been allowed by a blue ribbon Board of Appeals was deemed to endow them with a particularly strong presumption of validity.[35.1]

[35.1] Anchor Plastics Co. v. Dynex Plastics Corp., 363 F. Supp. 582, 587, 179 U.S.P.Q. 264, 268 (D.N.J. 1973), *aff'd* 492 F.2d 1238 (3d Cir. 1974).

[In same paragraph, add after footnote 36:]

At least one court has held that a preponderance of evidence is sufficient to establish invalidity.[36.1]

[36.1] Dickstein v. Seventy Corp., 522 F.2d 1294, 1297, 187 U.S.P.Q. 138, 140 (6th Cir. 1975).

[In same paragraph, add after footnote 38:]

While a prior ruling of patent validity does not create an estoppel of issues of fact against a person not before the court in the earlier case, it does substantially strengthen the statutory presumption of validity.[38.1] A litigant attacking the validity of a patent before a court that previously concluded that that patent was valid must show that there is a "material Distinction" between the present and prior cases.[38.2]

[38.1] Illinois Tool Works, Inc. v. Foster Grant Co., — F.2d —, —, 192 U.S.P.Q. 365, 367 (7th Cir. 1976).

[38.2] Mercantile National Bank of Chicago v. Howmet Corp., 524 F.2d 1031, 1032, 188 U.S.P.Q. 353, 354 (7th Cir. 1975), *cert denied.*

[In tenth text line of last paragraph on the page (paragraph running over to page 296), add after "injunctive relief.":]

Laches also bars a patentee from collecting damages for past infringement. Laches does not bar a patentee from collecting damages or obtaining an injunction for the period after suit is filed.[39.1] Laches, being an equitable defense, would not be available to willful infringers.[39.2]

[39.1] Siemens, A,G. v. Beltone Electronics Corp., 184 U.S.P.Q. 433, 438 (N.D.Ill. 1974).
[39.2] Bourns, Inc. v. Allen-Bradley Co., 182 U.S.P.Q. 258, 259 (N.D.Ill. 1974).

PAGE 296

[*Add immediately preceding first full text paragraph on the page:*]

No precedent declares at what point delay in bringing an infringement action becomes unreasonable. Each situation must be evaluated individually on its facts and circumstances. Patent owner's "other litigation" is only one of many factors to be considered when evaluating laches defense to an infringement action.[40.1] The existence of other litigation does not automatically excuse a delay in bringing suit against a second alleged infringer.[40.2] Where there are a number of infringers, a plaintiff can pick his target, but is under an obligation to notify the others that they are in range.[40.3]

[40.1] TWM Manufacturing Co. v. Dura Corp., 189 U.S.P.Q. 274, 278 (E.D.Mich. 1975).
[40.2] American Home Products Corp. v. Lockwood Mfg. Co., 483 F.2d 1120, 1122-23, 179 U.S.P.Q. 196, 197-98 (6th Cir. 1973).
[40.3] Advanced Hydraulics, Inc. v. Otis Elevator Co., 186 U.S.P.Q. 1, 3-4 (7th Cir. 1975); Jones v. Ceramco, Inc., 378 F. Supp. 65, 68, 184 U.S.P.Q. 75, 77 (E.D.N.Y. 1974) and 387 F. Supp. 940, 184 U.S.P.Q. 591, 592 (E.D.N.Y. 1974); Siemens, A.G. v. Beltone Electronics Corp., 184 U.S.P.Q. 433, 436 (N.D.Ill. 1974).

[*Add text at end of second full paragraph, after the words* "Section 271.":]

The first step in deciding patent infringement is to determine the patent's scope, which may be done by examining the claims language, prosecution history, and state of the prior art.[41.1]

[41.1] Summers v. Laubach, 191 U.S.P.Q. 114, 116 (D.Kan. 1974).

PAGE 297

[*In fifth text line of first full paragraph, add footnote* **44.1** *after* "claims.":]

[44.1] CTS Corp. v. Piher International Corp., 527 F.2d 95, 100, 188 U.S.P.Q. 419, 423 (7th Cir. 1975).

[Insert text between third and fourth full paragraphs:]

Ordinarily, infringement of method claims may not be avoided merely by making slight variations in apparatus.[44.2]

Where claim called for "forming a core" and the defendant purchased the core material from others, that defendant was deemed *not* to have infringed the claim.[44.3]

Where the last step of a claim calls for "heating the catalyst" and such step is performed by the defendant's customer rather than by the defendant, that defendant was deemed *not* to have infringed the claim. Defendant's customers were not his agents.[44.4]

Infringement may not be avoided by merely reversing or otherwise varying the steps in the process when the same result is accomplished in substantially the same way.[44.5]

[44.2] CMI v. Metropolitan Enterprises, Inc., 534 F.2d 874, 881, 189 U.S.P.Q. 770, 776 (10th Cir. 1976).

[44.3] Laminex, Inc. v. Fritz, 389 F. Supp. 369, 183 U.S.P.Q. 215 (N.D.Ill. 1974).

[44.4] Mobil Oil Corp. v. Filtrol Corp., 501 F.2d 282, 291-92, 182 U.S.P.Q. 641, 647-48 (9th Cir. 1974). Compare, Mobil Oil Corp. v. W.R. Grace & Co., 367 F. Supp. 207, 180 U.S.P.Q. 418 (D.Conn. 1973).

[44.5] Mobil Oil Corp. v. Filtrol Corp., 391 F. Supp. 337, 349, 183 U.S.P.Q. 258, 267 (C.D.Cal. 1974).

§ 2[1]. Doctrine of Equivalents

PAGE 298

*[In second text line on the page, add after sentence ending in footnote **46**:]*

Resort may be had to the specification to determine the intended meaning of a word used ambiguously in the claims.[46.1]

[46.1] Fay v. J.I. Case Co., — F. Supp. —, —, 191 U.S.P.Q. 210, 211 (N.D.Ohio 1976).

[Add text immediately preceding first full paragraph:]

The doctrine of equivalents is a principle peculiar to patent law whereby after all aids to interpretation are exhausted and claims' scope is enlarged as far as words can be stretched, courts make them cover more than their meaning will bear on proper occasions.[47.1] The broadest protection under the doctrine of equivalents is reserved for pioneer or generic patents, which cover a function never before performed, a wholly novel device, or one of such novelty and importance as to mark a distinct step in an art's progress as distinguished from a mere improvement or perfection of what had gone before. Liberality is the keynote of construction of a pioneer patent.[47.2]

[47.1] Capri Jewelry, Inc. v. Hattie Carnegie Jewelry Enterprises, 539 F.2d 846, 850, 191 U.S.P.Q. 11, 15 (2d Cir. 1976).

[47.2] Cathodic Protection Service v. American Smelting & Refining Co., 190 U.S.P.Q. 254, 268-69 (S.D. Tex. 1975).

PAGE 300

[Add text after quoted matter at top of page:]

Equivalency is established where a person reasonably skilled in the art would have known of the interchange-ability of an ingredient not disclosed in the patent with one that was disclosed.[50.1] Equivalency need not have been known at the time of the invention.[50.2] Equivalency would be measured at least with respect to the state of the art as it existed on the patent issue date, rather than on its filing date.[50.3]

[50.1] Lockheed Aircraft Corp. v. United States, — F.2d —, —, 190 U.S.P.Q. 134, 146 (Ct.Cl. 1976).

[50.2] Diamond International Corp. v. Maryland Fresh Eggs, Inc., 374 F. Supp. 1223, 1247, 182 U.S.P.Q. 147, 165 (D.Md. 1974).

[50.3] Laser Alignment, Inc. v. Woodruff Sons, Inc., 491 F.2d 866, 873, 180 U.S.P.Q. 609, 613 (7th Cir. 1974).

[Add text at end of the section:]

The rationale for the doctrine of equivalents was well expressed by the court in a recent case:

> If patents were interpreted only by the literal scope of their claims, however, minor deviations in the structure of almost any invention could be devised to elude the reach of the patent's protection. Thus, experience with patent cases demonstrates that seldom may the question of infringement be determined on the literal words of the claim. In recognition of the fact that a patent would be virtually worthless if it did not protect against devices which incorporate unimportant variations of the patented device, courts developed the doctrine of equivalents to protect the patentee from devices that differ merely in the name, form, or shape

from the patented invention, but perform substantially the same function in substantially the same way to obtain the same result.[51.1]

[51.1] Ziegler v. Phillips Petroleum Co., 483 F.2d 858, 868, 177 U.S.P.Q. 481, 487 (5th Cir.), *cert. denied* 414 U.S. 1079 (1973).

§ 2[2].   Doctrine of File Wrapper Estoppel

PAGE 301

[In last paragraph of the section, add text after sentence ending in footnote 55:]

A still further extension of the concept of file wrapper estoppel has been denominated "file wrapper estoppel by admission." Basically stated, file wrapper estoppel by admission is applicable where, after rejection, the applicant clarifies the meaning of a claim without rewriting the claim. The applicant will be bound by the limitation expressed in the clarification even though he does not seek to rely on the doctrine of equivalents.[55.1] Other courts have held that there is no file wrapper estoppel when language was added to the claims for purposes of clarification only.[55.2] A mere "semantic" change does not create file wrapper estoppel.[55.3] Where a Rule 312 Amendment altered a claim and also contained a statement to the effect that such modification of the claim did not depart from the scope of the invention as previously allowed, the patentee was estopped in litigation from asserting otherwise.[55.4]

[55.1] National Research Development Corp. v. Great Lakes Carbon Corp., 188 U.S.P.Q. 327, 336 (D.Del. 1975); Duplan Corp. v. Deering Milliken, Inc., 181 U.S.P.Q. 621, 627 (D.S.C. 1974).
[55.2] Swanson v. Unarco Industries, Inc., 479 F.2d 664, 670-71, 178 U.S.P.Q. 17, 22 (10th Cir. 1973), *cert. denied* 414 U.S. 1076 (1974).
[55.3] Laser Alignment, Inc. v. Woodruff & Sons, Inc., 491 F.2d 866, 876, 180 U.S.P.Q. 609, 615 (7th Cir. 1974).
[55.4] Parker v. Motorola, Inc., 524 F.2d 518, 533, 188 U.S.P.Q. 225, 237 (5th Cir. 1975).

§ 2[3].   Inverse Doctrine of Equivalents

PAGE 302

[Insert text between first and second paragraphs:]

Infringement is not proved merely by reading a claim upon the accused device, for infringement is not a mere matter of words. Even though claims of patent read to some extent upon the accused device, a court will look beyond the claims and consider the function and operation of devices themselves to determine if there is infringement. Accused apparatus that performs the same work that patented apparatus performs, but in a substantially different manner, accomplishing substantially improved result, is not equivalent of patented apparatus, and, lacking any individual elements of patented apparatus, does not infringe.[57.1] Not only must literal response to terms of a claim be shown to make out a case of infringement, but it must also be shown that the accused system does substantially the same work in substantially the same way to accomplish substantially the same result as the claimed system.[57.2]

[57.1] Harris v. NRM Corp., 191 U.S.P.Q. 643, 649 (N.D.Ohio 1976).
[57.2] Decca Ltd. v. United States, 188 U.S.P.Q. 167, 172 (Ct.Cl. 1975).

§ 3.   Declaratory Judgments and Counterclaims

PAGE 304

[*In last text paragraph of the section, add after sentence ending in footnote* **68:**]

Several elements must be considered in determining whether a justiciable controversy has been shown in a patent case: (1) the position of the declaratory judgment plaintiff; (2) the nature of the threat made against him; and (3) the party making the threat and whether his action can be attributed to the patent owner. Since a patent may act as a scarecrow in the art, courts tend to construe the justiciable controversy requirement with liberality.[68.1] Indirect as well as direct charges of infringement may be sufficient to support a declaratory judgment action challenging patent validity. An infringement charge against a foreign corporation with respect to imported goods creates a significant risk of suit to a domestic wholly-owned subsidiary that is the sole importer and distributor of its goods in the United States.[68.2]

[68.1] Wembley, Inc. v. Superba Cravats, Inc., 315 F.2d 87, 137 U.S.P.Q. 235 (2d Cir. 1963).
[68.2] Volkswagen of America, Inc. v. Engelhard Minerals & Chemicals Corp., 189 U.S.P.Q. 297 (S.D.N.Y. 1975).

[Add text at end of section:]

The holding in *Thiokol Chemical Corp. v. Burlington Industries, Inc.,*[69.1] that there is no federal jurisdiction to grant declaratory judgment of patent validity, scope, and noninfringement at the behest of licensee who faces impending state court royalty action, is of questionable force.[69.2]

An actual controversy exists between an accused infringer and a patent owner that sent three letters, which made implicit charges of infringement and thinly veiled threats to sue.[69.3] A patent owner's letter stating that manufacture and sale of devices would constitute infringement, even though patent owner stated that it did not know exact structure of devices, would cause reasonable apprehension and would be regarded as more than notice that license was unavailable.[69.4]

[69.1] 172 U.S.P.Q. 257.

[69.2] Hanes Corp. v. Millard, 531 F.2d 585, 189 U.S.P.Q. 331 (D.C.C. 1976).

[69.3] The Dayton Casting Co. v. Full Mold Process, Inc., 404 F. Supp. 670, 673, 190 U.S.P.Q. 336, 338 (S.D.Ohio 1975).

[69.4] Electro Medical Systems, Inc. v. Medical Plastics, Inc., 393 F. Supp. 617, 619, 188 U.S.P.Q. 591, 593 (D.Minn. 1975).

§ 4.   Some Consequences of Invalidity

PAGE 305

[Insert text between first and second full paragraphs on the page:]

Collateral estoppel does not apply to a mere holding of noninfringement. There must have been a determination of invalidity in the earlier litigation before collateral estoppel can be invoked.[72.1] A prior holding of validity, while it enhances the presumption of validity, is not conclusive and the presumption may still be rebutted in subsequent litigation.[72.2] Where fewer than all the claims have been held invalid, some courts hold that collateral estoppel applies only to those claims actually adjudicated.[72.3] Other courts hold that collateral estoppel applies to all the claims of a patent, even though only some had been invalidated in the earlier case.[72.4] It has been held that an agreement to pay a fixed sum in settlement of a past infringement remains enforceable notwithstanding an adjudication of invalidity or noninfringement.[72.5]

[72.1] Capri Jewelry, Inc. v. Hattie Carnegie Jewelry Enterprises, Ltd., 539 F.2d 846, 853, 191 U.S.P.Q. 11, 17 (2d Cir. 1976); General Plywood Corp. v. Georgia Pacific Corp., 504 F.2d 515, 517, 184 U.S.P.Q. 131, 133 (5th Cir. 1974); Ransburg Electro-Coating Corp. v. Spiller & Spiller, Inc., 304 F. Supp. 1385, 173 U.S.P.Q. 486 (S.D.Ohio 1972), *modified* 489 F.2d 974, 180 U.S.P.Q. 112 (7th Cir. 1973).

[72.2] Safe Flight Instrument Corp. v. McDonnell-Douglas Corp., 482 F.2d 1086, 178 U.S.P.Q. 13 (9th Cir. 1970), *cert. denied* 414 U.S. 1113 (1974); Columbia Broadcasting Systems, Inc. v. Zenith Radio Corp., 391 F. Supp. 780, 785-86, 185 U.S.P.Q. 662, 666 (N.D.Ill. 1975).

[72.3] Hickory Springs Mfg. Co. v. Fredmar Bros. Furniture Co., 509 F.2d 55, 184 U.S.P.Q. 459 (7th Cir. 1975); Bourns, Inc. v. Allen Bradley Co., 480 F.2d 123, 178 U.S.P.Q. 193 (7th Cir. 1973), *cert. denied* 414 U.S. 1094 (1974).

[72.4] Westwood Chemical, Inc. v. Molded Fiber Glass Body Co., 498 F.2d 1115, 182 U.S.P.Q. 517 (6th Cir. 1974); Technograph Printed Circuits, Ltd. v. Methode, Inc., 484 F.2d 905, 179 U.S.P.Q. 206 (7th Cir. 1973); Sampson v. Ampex Corp., 478 F.2d 339, 178 U.S.P.Q. 65 (2d Cir. 1973).

[72.5] Ransburg Electro-Coating Corp. v. Spiller, 489 F.2d 974, 180 U.S.P.Q. 112 (7th Cir. 1973).

PAGE 306

[*In second line of text on the page, add after sentence ending in footnote* 73:]

There is a split in authority as to whether a licensee can challenge patent validity after a consent decree between the parties. Some courts have held that a consent decree of patent validity precludes the accused infringer from afterwards attacking validity.[73.1] *Lear v. Atkins*[73.2] does not require that the courts answer every beck and call of the fickle suitor whose transient affection is governed by on-again, off-again strategies.[73.3] Other courts, however, have held that a consent decree does not preclude the accused infringer-licensee from afterwards attacking validity.[73.4]

A licensee may be estopped to contest the validity of his licensor's patent where he has engaged in fraudulent or unconscionable conduct.[73.5]

A licensee's covenant not to contest the validity of his licensor's patent is void and unenforceable and does not bar raising the issue of validity, either affirmatively or as a defense.[73.6]

[73.1] Schlegel Mfg. Co. v. King Aluminum Corp., 381 F. Supp. 649, 184 U.S.P.Q. 22 (S.D.Ohio 1974).

[73.2] 395 U.S. 653, 162 U.S.P.Q. 1 (1969).

[73.3] Aro Corp. v. Allied Witan Co., 531 F.2d 1368, 1373, 190 U.S.P.Q. 392, 396 (6th Cir. 1976).

[73.4] Crane Co. v. Aeroquip Corp., 504 F.2d 1086, 183 U.S.P.Q. 577 (7th Cir. 1974); Kraly v. National Distillers & Chemical Corp., 182 U.S.P.Q. 130 (7th Cir. 1974).

[73.5] Petersen v. Fee International, Ltd., 381 F. Supp. 1071, 1073, 182 U.S.P.Q. 264, 266 (W.D.Okla. 1974); Systron-Donner Corp. v. Sunstrand Data Control, Inc., 182 U.S.P.Q. 561, 564 (Cal.Super.Ct. 1974).

[73.6] Uniroyal, Inc. v. A.C. Industries, 185 U.S.P.Q. 522, 523 (N.D.Ga. 1975); Diematic Mfg. Corp. v. Packaging Industries, Inc., 381 F. Supp. 1057, 1060, 184 U.S.P.Q. 410, 412 (S.D.N.Y. 1974).

§ 5.   The Conduct of Patent Litigation

§ 5[1].   Subject Matter Jurisdiction

PAGE 306

[*In fifth text line of first paragraph of this section, add after* "copyright cases.":]

While the federal courts have exclusive jurisdiction of actions *arising under* federal patent and copyright laws, an action for royalties under a patent license is properly brought in a state court.[77.1] In deciding an action involving a patent license, a state court may pass upon the validity of any patent or patents involved.[77.2] State courts, though reluctant to proceed while the federal case is underway, will not restrain the parties from proceeding in the federal case.[77.3] Patent matters primarily concerned with either consensual relations or tortious wrongdoing may be tried in state courts, which may consider validity or infringement. Jurisdiction of a state court founded on contract or tort is not defeated merely because patent's existence, validity, or construction may be involved. An aggrieved competitor can sue for damages in state court, for trade libel and unfair competition. State law controls tort claim for deceit in the sale of patent rights, fraudulent inducement to forego asserting patent rights, and wrongfully delaying issuance of a patent.[77.4]

Enforcement of a patent infringement settlement agreement which contains a patent license is cognizable in federal court even in the absence of a diversity of citizenship. A patent infringement settlement agreement is more than a patent license even when the former rests on and is carried out by means of the latter.[77.5]

[77.1] American Technical Industries, Inc. v. Howard, 190 U.S.P.Q. 435 (N.Y.Sup.Ct., Westchester Cty. 1975).

[77.2] Consolidated Kinetics Corp. v. Marshall, 182 U.S.P.Q. 434 (Wash.Ct.App. 1974); Systron-Donner Corp. v. Sundstrand Data Control, Inc., 182 U.S.P.Q. 561 (Cal.Super.Ct. 1974).

[77.3] Acheson Industries, Inc. v. Wallace Clark & Co., 184 U.S.P.Q. 497 (Mich.Cir.Ct. 1974); Kollmorgan Corp. v. Shipley Co., 184 U.S.P.Q. 500 (N.Y.Sup.Ct. Nassau Cty. 1974).

[77.4] Miller v. Lucas, 191 U.S.P.Q. 166 (Cal.Ct.App., 2 Dist., Div.4, 1975).

[77.5] The Aro Corp. v. Allied Witan Co., 531 F.2d 1368, 1372, 190 U.S.P.Q. 392, 395 (6th Cir. 1976).

[*In tenth text line of same paragraph, add after sentence ending in footnote* **78**.*]

Twenty-eight U.S.C. Section 1338 jurisdiction does not require a minimum amount in controversy.[78.1]

[78.1] Enders v. American Patent Search Co., 535 F.2d 1085, 1088, 189 U.S.P.Q. 569, 573 (9th Cir. 1976).

PAGE 307

[*Add new section:* § **5[1][a]** *at end of* § **5[1]**.]

§ 5[1][a]. Jurisdiction over the parties

The legal titleholder of the patent is an indispensable party to a suit for the infringement of that patent.[79.1]

[79.1] Sims v. Mack Trucks, Inc., 407 F. Supp. 742, 743, 191 U.S.P.Q. 218 (E.D.Pa. 1976).

§ 5[2]. Venue

PAGE 307

[*Add text at end of section:*]

The more liberal provision of the general venue statute, 28 U.S.C. 1391, which allows an action to be brought in the district in which the claim arose, even though the defendant has no regular place of business there, and in the case of a corporation, in the district wherein it is incorporated or is licensed to do business or is doing business, is inapplicable to suits for patent infringement.[80.1]

An "act of infringement within the contemplation of 280 U.S.C. 1400(b)" has no narrowly defined parameters so that recourse must be had to the totality of the fact situation to determine whether accused infringer has, in that district, sufficiently impaired patent owner's rights. The fact that the accused infringer sold the accused device within the district may weigh in favor of concluding that venue is proper but would not be necessary.[80.2]

Accused infringer that systematically and continuously solicited orders and maintained a large showroom, including accused devices, which were demonstrated, committed acts of infringement in district within the meaning of 28 U.S.C. 1400(b).[80.3]

"Residence" within the meaning of 28 U.S.C. 1400(b) refers to the state of incorporation.[80.4]

[80.1] A.O. Smith-Inland, Inc. v. Hoeganaes Corp., 407 F. Supp. 539, 189 U.S.P.Q. 439 (N.D.Ill. 1976); "A" Company, Inc. v. Consyne Corp., 191 U.S.P.Q. 126 (S.D.Cal. 1975).

[80.2] B & J Manufacturing Co. v. FMC Corp., 191 U.S.P.Q. 32 (N.D.Ill. 1976).

[80.3] Dual Manufacturing & Engineering, Inc. v. Burns Industries, Inc., 531 F.2d 1382, 190 U.S.P.Q. 449 (7th Cir. 1976).

[80.4] Hunter v. FMC Corp., 190 U.S.P.Q. 66 (N.D.Ill. 1975).

§ 5[3]. Discovery

PAGE 307

[*In ninth text line of this section, add after sentence ending in footnote* **83***:*]

The fact that the cause of action is in the nature of a patent infringement makes little difference with regard to the general rule that ordinarily a defendant is entitled to examine the plaintiff in the forum where the plaintiff has chosen to sue.[83.1]

[83.1] Martin Engineering Co. v. Vibrators, Inc., 188 U.S.P.Q. 504, 505 (E.D.Ark. 1975).

§ 5[4]. Preliminary Injunction

PAGE 308

[*In fifth text line of this section, add after* "to the court's satisfaction."*:*]

Probability of irreparable harm was found insufficient to warrant a preliminary injunction requiring that evidence relating to a process which was the subject of a trade secret be taken in camera in a contempt trial against the trade secret licensee.[90.1]

[90.1] Stamicarbon, N.V. v. American Cyanamid Co., 506 F.2d 532, 183 U.S.P.Q. 321 (2d Cir. 1974).

§ 5[5]. Trial

PAGE 309

[*Add text at end of section:*]

The trier of fact is not bound to accept expert opinion, even if it is uncontradicted.[96.1] A file wrapper may not be permitted to be placed into evidence unless there is a witness available in the courtroom who is competent to explain it.[96.2]

The patent examiner who examined a patent involved in litigation is subject to compulsory testimony as to factual matters that do not invade his decision-making mental processes. In that patent examiners perform quasi-judicial duties their mental processes merit protection under the "mental processes rule."[96.3]

[96.1] Minnesota Mining & Manufacturing Co. v. Berwick Industries, Inc., 190 U.S.P.Q. 209, 211 (3d Cir. 1976).

[96.2] Mr. Hanger, Inc. v. Cut Rate Plastic Hangers, Inc., 372 F. Supp. 88, 91, 181 U.S.P.Q. 850, 852 (E.D.N.Y. 1974).

[96.3] Standard Packaging Corp. v. Curwood, Inc., 365 F. Supp. 134, 135-36, 180 U.S.P.Q. 235, 236 (N.D.Ill. 1973).

§ 5[6]. Appellate Review

PAGE 309

[*In seventh text line of this section, add after* "reviewable by the circuit courts.":]

The rules governing appellate review by courts of appeals in patent cases are no different than in other types of civil litigation.[98.1]

[98.1] Tights, Inc. v. Acme-McCrary Corp., 541 F.2d 1047, 1055, 191 U.S.P.Q. 305, 310 (4th Cir. 1976).

PAGE 309

[*Add new sections: §§ 5[7]-5[9] at end of chapter:*]

[7] Consent Judgment

Res judicata effect has been accorded a consent decree which adjudicated both validity and infringement issues.[101]

[8] Summary Judgment

Suits involving patent validity are not immune from disposition on motion for summary judgment.[102] However, summary judgment is to be granted cautiously in patent litigation, and only when it can be clearly concluded, after giving full weight to the opposing party's offerings, that there exists no genuine issue of material fact.[103] The impropriety of granting summary judgment in patent cases is compounded where forfeiture of the patent is sought on the basis of the patentee's personal misconduct in procuring the patent, as well as on technical and scientific facts.[104]

[9] Class Actions

Courts seem reluctant to allow actions against a "class" of infringers, primarily because of the diverse issues and adverse interests among the members of the would-be class.[105] The risk of inconsistent or varying adjudication, usually offered as a reason for allowing a class action, does not apply to patent litigation.[106]

[101] Wallace Clark & Co. v. Acheson Industries, Inc., 532 F.2d 846, 190 U.S.P.Q. 321 (2d Cir. 1976).

[102] NCR Corp. v. Eastman Kodak Co., 191 U.S.P.Q. 194, 199 (N.D.Ill. 1976).

[103] Spalding v. Antonions, — F.2d —, 191 U.S.P.Q. 593 (4th Cir. 1976).

[104] Pfizer, Inc. v. International Rectifier Corp., 538 F.2d 180, 185, 190 U.S.P.Q. 273, 277 (8th Cir. 1976).

[105] Dale Electronics, Inc. v. R.C.L. Electronics, Inc., 362 F. Supp. 130, 178 U.S.P.Q. 525 (D.N.H. 1972), aff'd 493 F.2d 1222, 182 U.S.P.Q. 76 (4th Cir. 1974); Sperberg v. Firestone Tire & Rubber Co., 61 F.R.D. 70, 178 U.S.P.Q. 566 (N.D. Ohio 1973). See also, Arneson v. Raymond Lee Organization, Inc., 59 F.R.D. 145, 179 U.S.P.Q. 210 (C.D.Cal. 1973).

[106] D. Klein & Son, Inc. v. Giant Umbrella Co., 179 U.S.P.Q. 34, 36 (S.D.N.Y. 1972).

Notes

PAGE 311

[Add to footnote 33:]

Parker v. Motorola, Inc., 524 F.2d 518, 521, 188 U.S.P.Q. 225, 227 (5th Cir. 1975).

[Add to footnote 36:]

Carter v. Rice, 398 F. Supp. 474, 188 U.S.P.Q. 451 (N.D.Tex. 1975).

PAGE 312

[Add to footnote 69:]

American Machine & Hydraulics, Inc. v. Mercer, 188 U.S.P.Q. 269 (C.D.Cal. 1975); Cryomedics, Inc. v. Spembley, Ltd., 397 F. Supp. 287, 188 U.S.P.Q. 255 (D.Conn. 1975).

[*Add to footnote* **72**:]

Kaiser Industries Corp. v. Jones & Laughlin Steel Corp., 515 F.2d 964, 185 U.S.P.Q. 343 (3d Cir. 1975), *rev'g* 181 U.S.P.Q. 193 (W.D.Pa. 1974); Catanzaro v. International Telephone & Telegraph, 378 F. Supp. 203, 183 U.S.P.Q. 273 (D.Del. 1974).

[*Add to footnote* **73**:]

American Sterilizer Co. v. Sybron Corp., 526 F.2d 542, 545, 188 U.S.P.Q. 97, 99 (3d Cir. 1975); Massilon-Cleveland-Akron Sign Co. v. Golden State Advertising Co., 444 F.2d 425, 170 U.S.P.Q. 440 (9th Cir.), *cert. denied* 404 U.S. 873 (1971).

[*Add to footnote* **76**:]

Nebraska Engineering Corp. v. Shivvers, — F. Supp. —, 191 U.S.P.Q. 682 (S.D.Iowa 1976).

PAGE 313

[*Add to footnote* **98**:]

ADM Corp. v. Speedmaster Packaging Corp., 525 F.2d 662, 664, 188 U.S.P.Q. 546, 547 (3d Cir. 1975).

Chapter 16

ELEMENTS OF TRANSNATIONAL PATENT LAW

§ 5. Later-Filed Patent Applications

PAGE 323

[*In ninth text line of first full paragraph on the page, add after* "for such treatment":]

More recently, the Commissioner of Patents has allowed an applicant to claim the benefit of a foreign priority application in a continuation application, even though neither a claim for priority had been made nor the priority document filed in the parent application.[19.1]

[19.1] *In re* Tangsrud, 184 U.S.P.Q. 746 (Comm.Pat. 1973).

[*In third text line of second full paragraph, add after* "is based.":]

To be established to U.S. patent protection, a specification must comply with U.S. disclosure requirements, whether or not the specification satisfies the disclosure requirements in the country in which it was first filed. The United States is not obliged by the Paris Union to give an application of foreign origin greater effect than would have been possible had it first been filed in the United States.[19.2]

[19.2] Kawai v. Metlesics, 480 F.2d 880, 178 U.S.P.Q. 158 (C.C.P.A. 1973).

PAGE 324

[*Add text immediately preceding first full paragraph on the page:*]

The right of priority is personal to the United States applicant; therefore, an application made by an inventor's assignee in a foreign country cannot be the basis for priority unless made on his behalf.[22.1]

[22.1] Vogel v. Jones, 486 F.2d 1068, 179 U.S.P.Q. 425, 428 (C.C.P.A. 1973).

[*Insert text between second and third full paragraphs:*]

However, it has been held that a British patent specification was prior art apparently as of the time it was filed in the United Kingdom Patent Office.[27.1]

[27.1] Triax Co. v. Hartman Metal Fabrications, Inc., 479 F.2d 951, 954, 178 U.S.P.Q. 142, 144 (2d Cir. 1973), *cert. denied* 414 U.S. 1113 (1974).

PAGE 328

[*Insert text between first and second full paragraphs on the page:*]

Some courts have relied upon the claims in counterpart (parallel) foreign applications to construe claims in the U.S. application.[36.1]

[36.1] Esso Research & Engineering Co. v. Kahn & Co., 379 F. Supp. 205, 183 U.S.P.Q. 582 (D.Conn. 1974); Jack Winter, Inc. v. Koratron Corp., 375 F. Supp. 1, 181 U.S.P.Q. 353 (N.D.Cal. 1974).

§ 7. Problems Arising From Importation and Exportation of Patented Goods

PAGE 330

[*In fourth text line of fourth full paragraph on the page, delete sentence beginning* "Thus, the failure . . ." *through end of paragraph. Substitute:*]

In the European Economic Community it has been held that the owner of parallel national patents may not use the ownership of separate national patents to exclude patented goods from entering one country of the Community where they were purchased from the patentee or his licensee in another country of the Community.[52.1] However, a national patent of one of the countries comprising the Community may be employed to exclude goods which were manufactured in another country of the Community, which other country does not afford patent protection for that type of invention.[53]

It has been held not improper for the patentee to forbid his foreign licensees from exporting the patented product to the United States.[53.1]

[52.1] Centraform BV v. Sterling Drug, Inc., 14 Comm.Mkt.L.R. 480, CCH Comm. Mkt. Rep. 8247 (Case No. 15/74, 1974).
[53.1] Dunlop Co., Ltd. v. Kelsey-Hayes Co., 484 F.2d 407, 417-18, 179 U.S.P.Q. 129, 136 (6th Cir. 1973), *cert. denied.*

[*In third text line of seventh full paragraph (still page 330), add after* "Tariff Act of 1930.":]

,and of Section 341 of the Trade Act of 1974 which amends Section 337 of the Tariff Act of 1930.

[*Also in third text line of seventh full paragraph, delete sentence beginning* "Accordingly, the Tariff Commission . . ." *through end of paragraph. Substitute:*]

The International Trade Commission (ITC) may, after conducting a hearing, issue a permanent exclusion order (19 U.S.C. 1337(d)) or a cease and desist order (19 U.S.C. 1337(f)). Cease and desist orders are enforced by the threat of an exclusion order in the event the offender fails to comply with the cease and desist order. The International Trade Commission is also empowered to issue temporary exclusion orders (19 U.S.C. 1337(e)). After the International Trade Commission has made a determination, the President has sixty days in which to approve or disapprove (19 U.S.C. 1337(g)).

Any person adversely affected by a final determination of the International Trade Commission has right of appeal to the United States Court of Customs & Patent Appeals. 19 U.S.C. 1337(c). However, an interlocutory order in relation to which the International Trade Commission has not completed its review and issued a written decision is not appealable to the Court of Customs & Patent Appeals under ordinary circumstances.[58] The United States Court of Appeals for the District of Columbia Circuit has refused to sanction federal district court review, under the Administrative Procedure Act, of action taken by the International Trade Commission.[58.1] When concurrent suits were brought for infringement under the Tariff Act, the court having jurisdiction of the infringement suit declined to enjoin the International Trade Commission from proceeding, as there had been no showing of irreparable harm.

In determining whether importation of goods which read on the claims of a subsisting United States patent constitute an unfair method of competition, the International Trade Commission must consider legal and equitable defenses (19 U.S.C. 1337(c)), including the possbile invalidity of the patent.[58.2]

---

[58] Import Motors Ltd. v. U.S. International Trade Commission, 530 F.2d 937, 188 U.S.P.Q. 102 (C.C.P.A. 1975).

[58.1] World Wide Volkswagen Corp. v. U.S. International Trade Commission, 414 F. Supp. 713, 191 U.S.P.Q. 626 (D.D.C. 1976).

[58.2] *In re* Chain Door Locks, 191 U.S.P.Q. 272 (U.S.I.T.C. 1976).

Notes

PAGE 332

[*Add to footnote* 1:]

Decca Ltd. v. United States, 191 U.S.P.Q. 439 (Ct.Cl. 1976).

[*Add to footnote* 5:]

Calvi v. Japan Airlines, Inc., 380 F. Supp. 1120, 184 U.S.P.Q. 293 (E.D.N.Y. 1974).

Chapter 17

COMPARATIVE PATENT LAW
SURVEY OF PRINCIPAL FOREIGN PATENT SYSTEMS

§ 8. A Comparison of Five Major Patent Systems

PAGE 351

[*Under "FEDERAL REPUBLIC OF GERMANY—WEST GERMANY," delete text of number "8" and substitute:*]

8. NON-STATUTORY SUBJECT MATTER: claims directed to compositions of matter are now permitted.